JEAN-PAUL SARTRE AND MORALITY

A LEGACY UNDER ATTACK

BEN WOOD JOHNSON

TESKO PUBLISHING
Pennsylvania

Copyright © 2017 by Eduka Solutions/Tesko Publishing
www.teskopublishing.com
330 W. Main St #214, Middletown, PA 17057 (United States of America)

Tesko Publishing is a division of Eduka Solutions and the Ben Wood Educational Consulting, LLC (a registered entity in Pennsylvania). It features works by Ben Wood Johnson. It highlights his goal towards excellence in research, scholarships, education, and philosophy. It promotes these works to readers worldwide.

© Ben Wood Johnson 2020 (Revised)

The author asserts his moral and legal rights

This work was first published in 2017

All rights reserved. No part of this publication may be reproduced, stored, distributed, or transmitted in any form or by any means, including photocopying, recording, or other electronic or mechanical methods, or by any information storage and retrieval system without the prior written permission of the publisher, except in the case of very brief quotations embodied in critical reviews and certain other noncommercial uses permitted by copyright law. Inquiries concerning the reproduction of this work beyond the scope of the terms and conditions listed above must be addressed to Ben Wood Educational Consulting, LLC at:

330 W. Main St #214, Middletown, PA 17057, United States of America

Published and printed in the United States of America by Tesko Publishing (An Independent Publishing House)

Paperback format

ISBN-13: 978-0-9979028-2-2 (paperback)
ISBN-10: 0-9979028-2-5 (paperback)

Cover design by Wood Oliver

Cover images
Copyright holder not raced. Any copyright concerned should be directed to the address listed above. If contacted by the copyright holder, the publisher would make the necessary adjustments and provide proper credits in subsequent reprints. Cover illustration by Wood Oliver. For more information about the author, visit his website at www.drbenwoodjohnson.com

For Gerunedan

Table of Contents

Preface ix
   Book Composition xiv
     The Sections xiv
     The Chapters xvi

Acknowledgments xix

Introduction 1
   Refuting Sartre 3

1. Introducing Jean-Paul Sartre 11
   Jean-Paul Charles Aymard Sartre 15
   Childhood 17
   Education and Personal Life 21

2. Profession & Career Trajectory 29
   Fame and Success 33
   Literary Contribution 36
   Recognition 38

3. A Political Idealist 43
   Sartre During World War II 44

Table of Contents

    The German Occupation 46
    A Political Activist 49

4. Les Temps Modernes 57

    Sartre After the War 59
    Freedom and Self-Identity 62
    Condemned to be Free 63

5. What is Ethics? 71

    Etymology of the Term Ethics 73
    The Features of Ethics 75
    Examining Approaches 77
    Paradigms of Ethics and Morality 78
    The Term Sartrean Ethics 81

6. The Authenticity Approach 87

    Why Examining Sartrean Ethics? 90
    Ownership of his Ethics 95
    A Neutral Approach 97

7. A Major Thinker 105

    An Introspective Tool 107
    Human Ontology and Ethics 112
    Community and Individual Values 115

8. A Prolific Writer 123

    Sartre and his Intimate Precepts 126
    Sartre's Role in Ethics 128
    Logistical Impediments 130

Summarizing Major Criticisms 132

9. Philosopher of the Century 141

The Basis of Sartrean Ethics 143
Morality and Freedom 147
Being and Non-Being 151

10. The Role of God 157

Temporality 160
Bad Faith [Mauvaise Foi] 162
Paths to Freedom 163

11. A Universal Thinker 167

Existentialism Under Attack 169
The Link Between Ethics and Freedom 171
Morality and Existentialism 173
Important Points of Dispute 176

12. Sartre and his Fewer Supporters 181

Linking Existentialism with Ethics 185
Mixed Reviews 187
A Philosophical Bequest 191
The Case for a Dual Approach 193
Achieving my Goals 195

Conclusion 201

Sartre is Still Alive 202
Central Thesis 207

Table of Contents

Bibliography **211**

A Prolific Writer **217**

Appendices **219**

Index **235**

About the Author **243**

Other Info **245**

Other Works **247**

TABLE OF FIGURES

Figure 8. 1: Sartre's three Ethics **125**

APPENDICES
Appendix A: Sartre's Major Works **221**
Appendix B: Publications While Alive............................**223**
Appendix C: Posthumous Publications **225**
Appendix D: Concepts And Quotes................................**225**
Appendix E: Famous Quotes..**227**

Preface

THIS BOOK EXAMINES the works that made Jean-Paul Sartre a famous philosopher. Although Sartre was a prolific writer and wrote extensively about a plethora of topics, the focus here is on his contribution to moral philosophy. Before we delve in the debate, let us explore Sartrean philosophy.

This book does not examine Sartre's entire literary repertoire. There are ample reasons for that. For example, many of Sartre's works are abstract. Others are complex. But on that basis alone, some critics sought to demote Sartre as a worthy

Preface

philosopher. I do not think this is a good way to establish Sartre's true literary valor.

This book relates only known facts about Sartre. It does not present fresh data about him. It does not elaborate on the life of this brilliant thinker. This is not a biography about Jean-Paul Sartre.

Despite these announced limits, there is a need to present an interesting case in Sartre's favor. The man contributed to several disciplines, including ethics. It is necessary to afford a more marked look to the ethical writings Jean-Paul Sartre produced both while alive and after he died.

Jean-Paul Sartre was an intellectual pillar. His works about phenomenology are without parallel. Just like his impetus in ontology, his role in moral philosophy is also incomparable.

Sartre was a controversial figure in modern-day literature. The most contentious facet of his works is his manner of exploring various issues, notably ethics. But there is more to Sartrean philosophy than most people realize. There is more to Sartrean ethics than most people would admit.

Regardless of popular opinions about Sartre's literary valor, he left a great heritage. Sadly, that legacy is under attack. Even though most critics hold a lesser esteem for Sartre, both as a person or as an influential thinker, countless others consider him a worthy contributor in literature. This book attempts to solidify that legacy.

This compilation does not refute the notion that most of Sartre's works are imperfect. As noted earlier, many of them are difficult to grasp. But the text offers a unique approach in the debate. It is important to note there is no consensus in the debate. Views are unclear about Sartrean ethics.

Some observers criticize Sartre relentlessly, more specifically in ethics. In criticizing his works in the domain, some are likely to undermine Sartre in every aspect. Although this may sound ludicrous, some critics refute the notion that Sartre was a pioneer in philosophy. They say that Sartre's works are not perfect. Is that the entire story? Probably not, I would say.

This work is about Sartrean ethics. Even so, it does not explore the issues in depth. If you would like to learn more about the subject, please visit my other works. They are listed toward the end of the document. You may see the text titled *Sartrean Ethics: A Defense of Jean-Paul Sartre as a Moral Philosopher*.

Preface

I will say this much though. Ethics is a complex concept. The notion has ramifications in other fields of study. Accordingly, we could appreciate the concept by exploring other issues.

The literature is laden with works that examine Sartre as a moral philosopher. Many of these works are one-sided, for they often look at the man from a narrow mindset. The popular claim is that Sartre did not publish a work on ethics while alive. This argument reflects the bias nature of the debate.

Critics seldom consider the works that Sartre compiled, but never released while alive. These works, I would argue, are the pillars of Sartrean ethics. Yet, some critics hold a lesser admiration for Sartre in the ethical domain.

While some people debate whether we should regard Sartre as a worthy contributor to ethics, others think that Sartre has an indisputable intellectual merit in the discipline. There is also the view that Sartre does not deserve any recognition in ethics because his works are disjointed. I disagree, although I am not the only person who sees the issues from this angle.

To reiterate, the present compilation is not concise; it is broader in scope. While it examines a few of the works Sartre produced about ethics, it explores the writings that made Jean-Paul Sartre an influential thinker. It revisits a few of the books Sartre released during his lifetime. They include publications about politics, novel, and psychology, to name a few. Here, I offer a superficial review of the Sartrean approach to moral philosophy.

This work is not exhaustive. But it is not a fruitless intellectual pursuit. While my arguments might seem trivial to some, the goal is to change the debate. I propose a daunting task here. The hope is to add a different side in the discourse.

Many critics see no relevance in Sartrean ethics. They might rebuke me as well. But these critics are in error. That being said, I do not intend to alienate dissenting viewpoints in the debate. Keep in mind that my position only reflects my understanding of the issues.

Anyway, I will echo that there is a need for a balanced approach in the debate. It is important to relate contradicting viewpoints. It is necessary to highlight the views that prominent scholars often echoed either for or against Sartrean ethics. It is pertinent to relate views echoed by bloggers, commentators, and other pundits.

Preface

I encourage productive criticisms in the debate. There is a need for civility and conviviality. The hope is that my appeal will not fall in deaf ears.

BOOK COMPOSITION

This book comprises three sections. They include: (1) *About Jean-Paul Sartre,* (2) *Sartrean Moral Identity,* and (3) *Ontology And Ethics*. Each section consists four chapters.

One section lays out the crux of the debate. The first few chapters introduce Jean-Paul Sartre. They outline a series of works, which are part of Sartre's literary repertoire. The book concludes with a bibliography and an index.[1]

THE SECTIONS

The first section is introductory. It outlines the fundamental ideas echoed throughout the text. This section draws attention to the events that

---

[1] Please note that the e-Book version does not include an index and appendices.

transpired during Sartre's personal growth and intellectual maturity. It outlines facts about Sartre's paths towards literary stardom, including his literary prowess and his political dissents.

The second section elaborates on the term ethics. It examines interpretations about this term. It addresses nuances between the term *"ethics,"* as a general terminology, and the term *"Sartrean ethics,"* as a narrower idea. This section centers on the materiality of Sartre's take on moral philosophy.

The third section assesses popular criticisms. An important goal is to make out whether we could consider Sartre a moral philosopher. An alternative goal is to offer evidence to support the notion that Sartre played a substantive role in moral philosophy.

The section explores: (1) the role of God; (2) the extent of existentialism in the way Sartre approached morality; and (3) the extent to which Sartrean ethics is rebuffed in the literature. The section outlines the views offered by several scholars to support Sartrean ethics.

The last section highlights important facts about Jean-Paul Sartre. It features several works, which Sartre published himself and other

Preface

publications, which had been released on his behalf. The section features memorable phrases and quotes, which Sartre used periodically during his long and successful career.

The Chapters

The manuscript comprises twelve chapters. Every chapter begins with a summary. Each of them lays out the major ideas recollected in the chapter. The goal is to promote a smooth reading experience.

The first chapter offers a review of the life of Jean-Paul Sartre. It provides a depiction of the man. It explores, though summarily, his childhood, his professional trajectory, and his accomplishments.

Chapters 2, 3, and 4 provide a review of Sartre's early life and professional trails. They recount facets of Sartre's « *parcours intellectuel.* » Chapters 5, 6, 7, and 8 dissect the term ethics. Chapter 9 notes that Sartre proved himself as a moral philosopher. Chapter 10 examines the Sartrean approach to ethics. Chapter 11 explores the link between human ontology and ethics. Chapter 12 explores mixed views about the intellectual relevance of Sartre's works about ethics.

Ben Wood Johnson

In sum, this book dissects the nature of Sartrean ethics, though it does so fleetingly. It reflects on certain facets of the literature. It relates works that criticize the Sartrean approach to morality. It also revisits publications that provide support for the notion that Sartre played a valuable role in ethics.

Preface

Acknowledgments

THIS WORK IS PART of a collection of essays I compiled many years ago. In 2015, I published a portion of the book. I titled it *"Sartrean Ethics: A Defense of Jean-Paul Sartre as a Moral Philosopher."*[2] This is an addendum to the previously noted work.

This opus is not an in-depth examination of the debate about Sartre. But it underlines the gist of a particular issue. This book is not thorough enough to offer an authoritative voice in the debate, for it

---

[2] Ben Wood Johnson, *Sartrean Ethics: A Defense of Jean-Paul Sartre As A Moral Philosopher* (Eduka Solutions, 2016).

Acknowledgements

references the views echoed by other scholars. Please refer to the publication referenced above to learn more about Sartrean ethics.[3]

I would like to thank the people who helped me in this project. I would like to thank Thomas Busch (from Villanova University). Dr. Busch put me on the right intellectual path. His expertise and his insights about Jean-Paul Sartre inspired this work.

I would like to thank Dr. Jacqueline Stefkovich for taking the time out of her busy schedule to review the manuscript. I would also like to thank my wife for lending me an added pair of eyes during editing. I would like to thank other contributors for their support. I appreciate their efforts in helping me polish this text.

January 27, 2017
Ben Wood Johnson, Ph.D.

Revised May 2020

---

[3] Johnson.

INTRODUCTION

JEAN-PAUL SARTRE was a popular philosopher. His fame extends in a wide range of subjects and fields of study. The fame that Sartre enjoyed (both while alive and post-mortem) is beyond presentation. This work alone could not describe the career of this influential thinker.

There is not a unique way of introducing Jean-Paul Sartre. His name is synonymous with literary excellence. The man was undeniably popular. The reputation of this acclaimed writer, thinker, and political activist is well settled. His intellectual valor is beyond authentication. At least, this is

Introduction

what most of us associate with the name Jean-Paul Sartre.

Few people know about an important side of Jean-Paul Sartre. He was a despised figure. Some say that Sartre was a polarized writer. Regardless of popular perceptions, Jean-Paul Sartre's fame is not without scrutiny. One particular fact about his literary legacy is regularly contested. That claim often comes from commentators and pundits who disagree with the notion that Sartre played a role in moral philosophy.

While I agree that certain facets of Sartre's literary legacy are worth debating, I do not think his works on ethics should be undermined or set aside for capricious reasons. Sartre's role in modern literature is irrefutable. His role in moral philosophy is also notable. While many people may disagree with his approach to ethics, there is a need for civility and conviviality in the debate.

Sartre should not be relegated to a status of ill repute in the fields of study that he excelled the most during his life. Granted, the Sartrean role in various disciplines is not perfect. His works in the domain of ethics are not that extensive.

Ben Wood Johnson

The Sartrean approach to a variety of literary disciplines, such as human ontology, is controversial. We should not refute his views by relying on unfounded reasons. On those grounds, I hope to defend facets of Sartre's literary legacy in ethics.

REFUTING SARTRE

Observers believe that Sartre was not a moral philosopher. What arguments they present to support that view? Opponents often point out that Sartre failed to lay down his relevance in ethics.

Others hold opposite viewpoints. These people have a much malleable opinion, while recognizing Sartre's shortcomings in ethical writings. From their vantage point, Sartre played a consistent role in ethics. They also noted that his works are uncompleted and fragmented. These viewpoints are worthy of further study.

Critics contain that the Sartrean ethical model was not all that it could be. I agree. But that does not mean that his works are empty of any intellectual relevance.

Introduction

While critics regard Sartrean ethics under a positive light, others are likely to minimize it. Some reject Sartre's role in the field completely. That is not fair to this brilliant thinker. I argue in favor of a conciliatory attitude in the debate.

Most commentators agree that Sartre did not present his ethical outline in the most coherent manner. Regardless, that is not enough to demote Sartre as a philosopher. It is likely that Sartre viewed himself as a moral philosopher. Shockingly, most observers share a similar outlook.

Most scholars recognize that the Sartrean ethical model is in fragments; at least, it is incomplete. Still, few of these intellectuals would deny that Sartre deserves merit for his contribution to the field. Many of the people who looked at Sartre's works accept that Sartrean ethics exists, though it is incomplete. That ethics, I would echo, is worthy of note here.

The present edition goes in a similar direction. It notes that Sartre has relevance in ethics. We should not undermine that relevance haphazardly.

Sartre was a mastermind in philosophy. His expertness in various philosophical ideas extends beyond ethics. But ethical notions, I would argue, are part of the Sartrean model of philosophy. It is apparent in phenomenology. There could not be one (that is, ethics) without the other (that is, ontology).

The preceding view might be in the minority. Even so, we could not lessen its intellectual potency. While I do not share popular assumptions about Sartre, I do not intend to defend Sartrean ethics out of passion. I will evoke evidence to support my arguments.

The goal is to defend Sartrean ethics as cogently as possible. That ethics exists, although I would admit that it is in an embryonic stage. Even so, Sartre approached ethics and human ontology in tandem; we must do the same.

The next sections and the upcoming chapters offer persuasive arguments in favor of Jean-Paul Sartre. They explore facets of the literature, including Sartre's own writings, to support my arguments. They relate the works by various scholars in the field as evidence.

The arguments proposed here emanated from several viewpoints, including personal reflections,

Introduction

class notes, lectures,[4] and non-academic materials. To echo, I approach the topic differently in this edition.[5] I encourage critics to do the same.

I propose a clear nomenclature about Jean-Paul Sartre's role in moral philosophy. I reckon that many people might refute the views expressed throughout this document. But my goal is not to convince every reader of Sartre's ethical talent. In short, to reiterate a previous assertion, the hope is to add a fresh stream in the debate.

---

[4] I attended Dr. Thomas W. Busch's course in the spring of 2014 (Villanova University). Please see chapter 16 for more information regarding this experience.

[5] Johnson, *Sartrean Ethics*.

SECTION 1

ABOUT JEAN-PAUL SARTRE

This section introduces Jean-Paul Sartre. It relates his acclaimed works and other accomplishments. The chapters explore Sartre's contribution to literature. They examine the extent of his intellectual repertoire, including materials that Sartre published during his lifetime and materials published on his behalf after he passed away. The chapters explore Sartre's major achievements, including his literary prowess, his political efforts, and his approach to fame and success. This section elaborates on Sartre's rise to fame, including his handling of his newly found success and recognition.

Chapter One

The Biography of Jean-Paul Sartre

This chapter presents a candid portrait of Jean-Paul Sartre. The aim is to assess Sartre's trajectory towards literary stardom. It explores his childhood, his education, his personal life, and his career choices. The discussions outlined here examine Jean-Paul Sartre as a man, a writer, and as a political activist. The chapter examines, although briefly, Sartre's upbringing, his humble beginning, and his professional achievements.

1. Introducing Jean-Paul Sartre

WHO WAS JEAN-PAUL Sartre? Why his approach to ethics matters? Answering these questions should not be a challenge. Most students of contemporary philosophy[6] know something about

---

[6] Contemporary philosophy is the period, which is marked by the professionalization of the discipline. This period in the history of Western philosophy is also marked by the rise of analytic and continental philosophy

Chapter 1: Introducing Jean-Paul Sartre

this important thinker in French literature.[7] Sartre was a legendary figure in various fields of study, including literature, psychology, and politics.

Jean-Paul Sartre was a global figure. He often took unpopular positions against important events in world affairs. For instance, during the Algerian War (1954), Sartre espoused a radical stance against this military escapade. Sartre loudly asserted his contempt for what he sensed as the effects of colonialism in the region.[8] Sartre was also vocal on events occurring in various parts of the world.[9]

The latter question could be harder, if not more complicated, to decipher. Two reasons are worth mentioning here. First, there is a growing debate about the applicability of Sartre's writings in ethics. While few people share the view that Sartre is a moral philosopher, most scholars in ethics reject that viewpoint. For them, Sartre has no intellectual

---

[7] "Contemporary Philosophy," *Wikipedia, the Free Encyclopedia*, May 21, 2015,
https://en.wikipedia.org/w/index.php?title=Contemporary_philosophy&oldid=663373229.

[8] David Drake, "Sartre, Camus and the Algerian War," *Sartre Studies International* 5, no. 1 (1999): 16–32.

[9] Sartre took bold positions about issues occurring in Cuba, Vietnam, and the United States, to name a few.

merit in the ethical discipline. Of course, this is a point of contention.

The second reason is that claims against Sartrean ethics can be unclear. Observers do not refute the idea that Sartre had an influence in moral philosophy. But they habitually question the extent of his works in the domain. This reflects the essence of the debate, which I propose to examine closer.

Should we or should we not recognize Sartre as a moral philosopher. I would say yes we should. But others might beg to differ. While some commentators recognize that Sartre played a role in moral philosophy, they are likely to examine, painstakingly at times, the importance of that role. They can be ambivalent in their positions.

Other analysts are harsher in their criticisms. They question the weight of the Sartrean approach to moral philosophy altogether. From their vantage point, Sartre has no intellectual merits in this discipline. I do not agree with such criticisms.

A major point of conflict in the debate is the publication argument. For critics, Sartre did not publish enough works, which outlined his ethical

Chapter 1: Introducing Jean-Paul Sartre

dimensions.[10] There is a need to question criticisms that rely only on such grounds. To repeat, this is the essence of the present publication.

Despite the contentious nature of Sartre's role in ethics, the common belief, at least in some circles, is that Sartre was an unparalleled thinker. His scrutiny of contemporaneous issues has seldom contested, though his methods and conclusions are often rebuked. Few people could deny that Sartre produced many works, which, for many years, guide human civilizations.

Through his writings, Jean-Paul Sartre influenced intellectual investigations in philosophy across many cultures. At any rate, Sartre's philosophical relevance is settled. This is so even though dissenters always seek to undermine the Sartrean legacy. Let us intimate ourselves with Jean-Paul Sartre. Let us discover the man at a personal level.

---

[10] Johnson, *Sartrean Ethics*.

Ben Wood Johnson

JEAN-PAUL CHARLES AYMARD SARTRE

The popular philosopher we know mostly as Sartre was born in Paris, France, on June 21, 1905. He is famously known as Jean-Paul Sartre. But his birth name is *Jean-Paul-Charles-Aymard-Léon-Eugène Sartre*. He was fondly known as "Poulou," his childhood nickname.[11]

Sartre was the only child of Anne-Marie Schweitzer (Mother) and Jean-Baptiste Sartre (Father). His father (Sartre Senior) was an officer in the French Navy (Ensign). Jean-Baptiste was on duty overseas during the time the young *Poulou* « Le Jeune Poulou » was born.[12] It is not clear whether Jean-Baptiste ever saw his son's face. He passed away from an unfortunate illness. However, it is clear that the *little Sartre* never knew his father.

While on duty, Sartre senior contracted a fever, from which he eventually died at the age of 30.[13] The young Poulou was still a baby when his father

---

[11] Thomas R. Flynn, *Sartre: A Philosophical Biography* (Cambridge: Cambridge University Press, 2014).

[12] Flynn.

[13] Flynn.

Chapter 1: Introducing Jean-Paul Sartre

passed away. Jean-Baptiste died only fifteen months after Anne-Marie had given birth to the little Jean-Paul or « *Le Petit Jean-Paul.* »

Sartre resented his father for leaving him so early in his life. He wondered whether Jean-Baptiste's passing was either a good thing or a bad thing for him. He struggled with the idea that his father might have been an impediment to his own development as both a human being and an intellectual.[14]

In the book titled « *Les Mots,* » Sartre wrote that his father went to hide in his death. Sartre was disappointed that he never had the opportunity to know him well. He writes:

« En flint à l'anglaise, Jean-Baptiste m'avait refusé le plaisir de faire sa connaissance. Aujourd'hui encore, je m'étonne du peu que je sais sur lui ».[15]

Translation

"By taking the French leave, Jean-Baptiste deprived me the pleasure of making his

---

[14] J.-P. Sartre, *Les Mots,* 1St Edition edition (Librairie Gallimard, 1964), 11.

[15] Sartre, 12.

acquaintance. To this day, I am surprised to see how much I still know about him."[16]

Despite the absence of his biological father, Sartre found a role model in his grandfather (Mother side). Sartre notes that his grandfather showed no reluctance in taking care of him. Sartre also notes that his grandmother was pleased to have him under her care.[17]

Jean-Paul Sartre grew up under the watchful eyes of his mother and other relatives. Granted, to the greatest extent, his upbringing was relegated to his grandparents. The following pages recount some crucial events that transpired during the childhood of Jean-Paul Sartre.

CHILDHOOD

Jean-Paul Sartre spent most of his life between « *Saint-Germain-des-Pres* » and « *Mont-parnasse.* » Until the age of ten, he was reared by his grandfather. In his autobiography (*Les Mots*), Sartre detailed his youth, with a tone of serenity. He

---

[16] Sartre, 12.

[17] Sartre, 9.

Chapter 1: Introducing Jean-Paul Sartre

depicted the life of his mother, a young widow in her early twenties, as intensely depressing and despondent.

After the death of his father, life, it would seem, took an unexpected turn for both Sartre and his mother (Anne-Marie). He writes:

« À la mort de mon père, Anne-Marie et moi, nous nous réveillâmes d'un cauchemar commun ; je guéris ».[18]

Translation

"After the death of my father, Anne-Marie and I had awoken from a common nightmare, from which I am cured."

Sartre notes that everything went downhill from that point forward in his life. He also notes that his mother had a hard time finding her way in the world. Anne-Marie moved to her parent's house. But Sartre suggests that Anne-Marie was not pleased of the treatment she received there.

While her parents opened their doors for Sartre's mother, she lost her liberty in exchange. Sartre writes:

---

[18] Sartre, 9.

« La mort de Jean-Baptiste fut la grande affaire de ma vie : elle rendit ma mère à ses chaines et me donna la liberté ».[19]

Translation

"The death of Jean-Baptiste was the story of my life; it cost my mother her freedom and gave me mine."

To survive away from her parent's control, Anne-Marie felt the need to find work outside her comfort zone. Because she did not have a profession, she held menial jobs. She worked as a nurse, an escort girl, a servant, a housekeeper, and a majordomo or steward.[20]

Sartre told everything about his past in « *Les Mots.* » He wrote this magnificent piece of literature around the 1950s. He later changed the work and published it in 1963.[21]

Sartre did not sound too thrilled about this epoch in his life. He described this experience as a

---

[19] Sartre, 11.

[20] Sartre, 10.

[21] Douglas Johnson, "A Born-Again Writer," *The Guardian*, October 30, 1987, http://www.theguardian.com/books/1987/oct/30/biography. This autobiography earned Sartre a Nobel Prize for literature, which he subsequently refused.

Chapter 1: Introducing Jean-Paul Sartre

dull or depressing childhood. Sartre did not have many friends as a child. He was excruciatingly shy. Sartre seldom engaged his peers. Sartre wrote in the mentioned publication that he spent most of his past years with an old man and two women (Sartre autobiography, « *Les Mots* » or *"The Words"* (1964).[22]

Sartre did not depict his childhood as a *"Romanesque"* experience. He lacked companionship from the other children of his own age. Sartre was not a happy child. He drifted into isolation and loneliness for a good portion of his childhood.

At a young age, Sartre dedicated himself to a life of reading and writing. Despite being shy and reserved, he was considered a brilliant student. Sartre first expressed an academic interest in psychology. In one of his early works, he dedicated his writings to childhood development.[23] In 1938, Sartre published a short story titled *"Childhood of a Leader"* or « *L'Enfance d'un Chef.* »[24]

---

[22] Jean-Paul Sartre, *The Words: The Autobiography of Jean-Paul Sartre*, First Edition (Braziller, 1964).

[23] Flynn, *Sartre*.

[24] Flynn.

Sartre considered a career in philosophy. He attended the Lycée Henri IV. He later attended « *Lycée Louis-le-Grand de Paris* » (between 1922 and 1924). The same year (in 1924), Sartre enrolled at the « *École Normale Supérieure,* » where he exceeded with zeal in his academic efforts. He had just turned nineteen.

EDUCATION AND PERSONAL LIFE

Sartre graduated from the École Normale Supérieure in 1927 with a degree in philosophy. He had just turned twenty-two years old.[25] But it would take another two years before Sartre could pass the state examination, which he did in 1929. The same year, Sartre met Simone de Beauvoir, whom would play an important role in his life.[26]

---

[25] The École Normale Supérieure is a French higher education establishment. Its structures are somewhat similar to the French public university systems. But its framework is unique in many facets.

[26] Simone de Beauvoir (1908-1986) is considered as Sartre's companion. Although they were not officially married, it is believed that, they initially had a romantic relation, which transformed in a life-long friendship, both intellectually and personally.

Chapter 1: Introducing Jean-Paul Sartre

There was an extraordinary personal and intellectual link between Sartre and Beauvoir.[27] They grew out of adolescent and into adulthood around the same era. They eventually matured together in both their personal and professional lives.

It is not clear how Sartre and Beauvoir became good friends. The nature of their friendship is a mystery to most. Even Beauvoir provided little details about her rapport with Sartre in her writings.[28] Still, it is often speculated that the pair enjoyed a romantic relationship before becoming inseparable friends.

According to Deirdre Bair, Beauvoir and Sartre became a couple around October 1929, when the two were confronted by Beauvoir's father. Sartre immediately sought to enter a matrimonial relationship with Beauvoir, which she refused. Instead, she opted for an open-ended liaison, which

---

[27] Kate Fullbrook and Edward Fullbrook, *Simone de Beauvoir and Jean-Paul Sartre: The Remaking of a Twentieth-Century Legend* (Harvester Wheatsheaf, 1993).

[28] Simone de Beauvoir published several books and, in many of them, she mentioned her link with Jean-Paul Sartre. She provided little details regarding her supposed romantic link with Sartre.

allowed them to see other people, both male and female.[29]

Others pointed out that the pair led a sexually diametrical life. Many people believe that Beauvoir was a bisexual,[30] while Sartre was a womanizer.[31] It is worthy of note that this avowal of Simone de Beauvoir often goes unmentioned.[32] Observers argue that, in some circles, there is a certain reluctance to portray or perhaps to *"frame"* Beauvoir as bisexual.[33]

Several commentators, including Hazel Rowley, claimed that Sartre and Beauvoir enjoyed an on-and-off romantic affair for many years.[34] It is also speculated that Beauvoir was not thrilled with

---

[29] Deirdre Bair, *Simone de Beauvoir: A Biography* (Simon and Schuster, 1991).

[30] Mariam Fraser, *Identity Without Selfhood: Simone de Beauvoir and Bisexuality* (Cambridge University Press, 1999).

[31] Fullbrook and Fullbrook, *Simone de Beauvoir and Jean-Paul Sartre*.

[32] Maria Pramaggiore and Donald E. Hall, *RePresenting Bisexualities: Subjects and Cultures of Fluid Desire* (NYU Press, 1996).

[33] Pramaggiore and Hall.

[34] Hazel Rowley, *Tete-a-Tete: The Tumultuous Lives and Loves of Simone de Beauvoir and Jean-Paul Sartre* (New York: Harper Perennial, 2006).

Chapter 1: Introducing Jean-Paul Sartre

this arrangement. She patently suffered deeply from jealousy, they say.

Simone De Beauvoir was torn, some say. While she wanted to be with Sartre, she also wanted to be free from his control. Observers argue that Beauvoir had mixed feelings about the liaison because "she wanted to keep the image of a model life intact."[35] But the understanding is that Beauvoir could not uphold a healthy liaison with Sartre, while being a leading figure in the woman's liberation movement.

Apart from the gossip, many believe that Sartre and Beauvoir's unrestricted bond was not by chance. Simone de Beauvoir became Sartre's loyal companion. They enjoyed a long and respectful rapport; they were joined to the hip. She stood by his side, both professionally and personally. They also enjoyed a lifelong intellectual relationship, although Beauvoir is regarded as "the driving

---

[35] Lisa Appignanesi, "Did Simone de Beauvoir's Open 'marriage' Make Her Happy?," *The Guardian*, June 10, 2005, sec. World news, http://www.theguardian.com/world/2005/jun/10/gender.politicsphilosophyandsociety.

intellectual power in the joint development of the couple's most influential ideas."[36]

Around 1934, Jean-Paul Sartre entered higher education. He became a teacher and, later, taught philosophy at the « *Lycée du Havre,* » in Paris. Sartre would later renounce this position in 1942.

Most observers do not know the reason that Sartre abandoned his teaching career. However, critics speculated that Sartre did so because he wanted to devote himself to full-time writing. Between 1933 and 1934, Sartre studied under the professorship of Edmund Husserl and Martin Heidegger at the « *Institut Français,* » in Berlin, Germany.

It is important to note that both Husserl and Heidegger were indisputable figures in Western philosophy. Overtime, Sartre refined his skills and became a powerhouse in philosophy. I will discuss this facet of his literary prowess later.

Unlike Husserl and Heidegger, Sartre made a bigger dent in contemporary philosophy with his own approach to phenomenology, which is centered on the individual's capacity to cultivate

---

[36] Fullbrook and Fullbrook, *Simone de Beauvoir and Jean-Paul Sartre*, 3.

Chapter 1: Introducing Jean-Paul Sartre

specific reality of consciousness.[37] Let us discuss this facet of Sartre's approach to philosophy as we move further in the manuscript.

---

[37] Alain D. Ranwez, *Jean-Paul Sartre's Les Temps Modernes, a Literary History, 1945-1952* (Whitston Pub. Co., 1981).

Chapter Two

Profession and Literary Successes

This chapter explores the characteristics of Jean-Paul Sartre, notably as an intellectual. It examines his professional trajectory, his fame, his success, his outmost literary contributions to the world, and his recognition. It explores how Sartre viewed himself and how he made out the world outside his personal bubble. It recounts Sartre's rejection of a Nobel Prize in 1964 and other recognitions.

2. Profession & Career Trajectory

SARTRE IMMERSED HIMSELF in the study of major philosophical principles. He became attracted toward a particular field. Sartre concentrated his research on the philosophical doctrine known as phenomenology.[38] During his

---

[38] Phenomenology is the study of experience through perception.

academic crucible, he held a professorship at the « *Lycée Condorcet,* » in Paris (1935-1942).[39]

Jean-Paul Sartre succeeded a major feat in his career. He is regarded as the father of the popular philosophical doctrine known as *"Existentialism."* Sartre also received credit as one of the leading figures in the tendency known as *"Phenomenology."*

Sartre became famous, notably for many of his intellectual accomplishments. For most observers, Sartre was a multi-faceted writer. Among his many talents, many people knew Sartre as a political critic or activist.[40] He was also known as a moralist, playwright, dramatist, novelist, and author of biographies and short stories.[41]

Jean-Paul Sartre did not have biological children. But in 1964, he adopted Arlette Elkaïm, a young woman (twenty-nine year old at the time) of Jewish-Algerian origin, who was studying

---

[39] Jean-Paul Sartre, *Being and Nothingness*, trans. Hazel E. Barnes, Reprint edition (New York: Washington Square Press, 1993).

[40] Thomas R. Flynn, *Sartre: A Philosophical Biography* (Cambridge: Cambridge University Press, 2014).

[41] Thomas R. Flynn, *Sartre: A Philosophical Biography* (Cambridge: Cambridge University Press, 2014).

philosophy.[42] Critics often talked about the secrecy that surrounded this adoption. Observers often note that Mrs. Elkaïm was among Sartre's many young fans before becoming his protégé and eventually his legal daughter.

On April 15, 1980, Sartre died in Paris. He was 74 years old. He was buried on April 19 of the same year. His funeral at first drew a crowd of twenty-thousand people gathered outside the « *Broussais Hospital.* » But the crowd grew to circa fifty-thousand (present); they marched through Paris.[43]

On the record, "There was no service; there were no speeches in Sartre's funeral."[44] However, it was a powerful farewell for this giant in literature. Sartre's passing was mourned in various circles across the globe.

---

[42] "Arlette Elkaïm-Sartre (1/5) - Littérature - France Culture," accessed August 8, 2015, http://www.franceculture.fr/emission-a-voix-nue-arlette-elkaim-sartre-15-2013-06-03; "Arlette Elkaïm-Sartre," *Babelio*, accessed August 8, 2015, http://www.babelio.com/auteur/Arlette-Elkaim-Sartre/59219.

[43] Jonathan Judaken, *Jean-Paul Sartre and the Jewish Question: Anti-Antisemitism and the Politics of the French Intellectual* (U of Nebraska Press, 2006).

[44] Judaken, 2.

Chapter 2: Profession and Career Trajectory

Sartrean philosophy still resounds throughout the literary world. For most admirers, Sartre is alive. Sartre *lives on* through his literary accomplishments. Observers echoed that Sartre is a definitive point of reference and an intellectual master.[45]

Critics have also pointed out a little ungratefulness towards Jean-Paul Sartre's literary accomplishments. Some say that there is a painstaking effort underway to rebuff that Sartre brought an enormous contribution to popular culture and literature.[46] Critics are quick to dismiss Sartrean philosophy, labeling it as difficult and rambling. I will discuss criticisms in more detail in Chapter 12.

Many people knew Sartre as a polemicist. They regarded him as a great intellectual. In 1938, Sartre published his first novel titled, « *La Nausée* » or "*Nausea.*" In this work, Sartre laid down the ground for his ideas about existentialism. In 1939, Sartre published a series of short essays titled, « *Le*

---

[45] Rachid Sabbaghi, "Sartre," *UNESCO Courier*, September 1, 1992, 31.

[46] Ibid.

Mur » or *"The Wall,"* which solidified his literary talents.

Most commentators regard Sartre as a controversial figure in French literature. Many accused him of being egotistical and inaccessible. Some even criticized his philosophy for being, what they note as, hard to digest intellectually. Much of Sartre's major works is written in a rambling style, many skeptics note.[47] In later chapters, I will examine the major disagreements that are often levied against Sartre.

FAME AND SUCCESS

Sartre is much within the stratum of leading thinkers, and unquestionably the most recognizable figures, of contemporaneous philosophy. He is perhaps a transcendent intellectual figure in the West. Observers, admirers and critics alike, believe that Sartre is the most significant thinkers in

---

[47] Edward Aloysius Pace and James Hugh Ryan, *The New Scholasticism* (American Catholic Philosophical Association, 1970).

Chapter 2: Profession and Career Trajectory

Western philosophy. Most would agree that Sartre is among notable writers in recent memory.

Jean-Paul Sartre's consent to fame and recognition went beyond the era when he was actively producing literary works. Observers argue that Sartre had a significant impact on human civilization and popular cultures. His ideas influenced many generations of thinkers or political philosophers alike.

Some commentators are quick to place Sartre among the prominent innovators in history. For admirers, Sartre is alive or as it is often referred to in various circles: « *Sartre n'a jamais cessé d'être vivant* ».[48] Thomas Flynn notes Jean-Paul Sartre as one of the preeminent philosophers of the twentieth century.[49] This sentiment is well known in various literary circles. Nonetheless, that view is mainly prevalent among admirers.

Sartre's place in the Pantheon of great contributors to literature is undisputable. He revolutionized the way human beings can examine themselves, both individually and in communities.

---

[48] Juliette Simont, Écrits posthumes de Sartre, II: avec un inédit de Jean-Paul Sartre (Vrin, 2001).

[49] Flynn, *Sartre*.

To this day, Sartre enjoys a significant literary legacy in human history. Despite criticisms, Sartre's works survived the test of time.

Critics note a phobia in Jean-Paul Sartre of not being able to match his potentials. Jean-Pierre Boulé looked at a piece of literature, which Sartre wrote when he was seventeen. In the piece, Sartre depicted a character that happened to be a teacher, was struggling to control his students. The character was a writer; but he was not successful. His only sense of power came from dominating a sick woman.

Boulé asked whether this piece sketched Sartre's own fear for failure.[50] The answer is not that obvious, as Boulé, himself, did not provide any. It is undeniable that Sartre contributed enormously to human literature. Whether Sartre wished fame, he became a household name. But he had to deal with the recognition, the prestige, and, of course, the lack of privacy that come with such a position.

---

[50] Jean-Pierre Boulé, *Sartre, Self-Formation, and Masculinities* (Berghahn Books, 2005), 78.

Chapter 2: Profession and Career Trajectory

LITERARY CONTRIBUTION

Sartre was not just a philosopher in the most basic meaning of the word *"Philosopher."* His ideas transformed both the individual and society (for example, collectively). Even after his death, Sartre continued to influence philosophical writings. Because Sartre published several posthumous works, he never stopped being relevant.[51]

The ambit of the Sartrean intellectual wealth is infinite. His most recent works, which had been made available by his adoptive daughter,[52] suggest that Sartre nourished the wish to leave his thoughts uncompleted.[53] Arguably, Sartre wanted his philosophy to remain open-ended. Based on what we know about the works Sartre produced, he wanted these works to remain without closure.

Sartre's intellectual prowess is unparalleled. His ontological dimensions are without comparisons.

---

[51] Simont, Écrits posthumes de Sartre, II.

[52] Johnson, "A Born-Again Writer."

[53] Arlette Elkaim-Sartre is the adopted daughter of Jean-Paul Sartre. She was a 19-year-old Jewish Algerian girl when Sartre met her in 1956.

Ben Wood Johnson

Jean-Paul Sartre is among the greatest thinkers of the past, present, and perhaps the future.

The Sartrean contribution to human literature is solidified through his writings about morality. But his views in this discipline are often refuted. We could understand the Sartrean approach to ethics as the source of many positions against Sartre himself.

A Sartrean role within the ethical realm often produces passionate debates and countless criticisms against both the man and his works. The extent of his publications about ethics is rebuffed. The chief constituency of his approach to the field is rejected.

I do not understand why critics abound from all angles against the Sartrean take on ethics. It is important to examine the essence of popular dissents against Sartre. There is a need to examine popular criticisms against his approach to morality.

Not only Sartre's ideas are the subject of constant scrutiny, his major philosophical theories are also the subject of intense debates. But Sartre continues to speak to us via both the works that he published himself and the works published on his behalf. Sartre's notions about ontology, discernibly

Chapter 2: Profession and Career Trajectory

his theory about human existence, are still relevant on the intellectual realm.

The ideas that Sartre interjected in modern philosophy and human thinking are unparalleled. The works he produced, supremely via *"Existentialism,"* played a large role in turning him into a polyvalent writer. Sartre is a creative philosopher.

Recognition

Although Jean-Paul Sartre gained enormous success, he did not seem consumed by his fame. He seemed unmoved by his increasingly dominant literary standing in the world. Sartre embraced fame and success with joy. Few hints suggest that he was uncomfortable or exasperated by his celebrity status.

Sartre projected a lackadaisical attitude about his newly earned fame and, to some extent, his intellectual reputation. His apparent lack of interest might not have been the result of his idiosyncrasies or conservative personality. Rather, it was perhaps the results of his ideology or his hyperbolic views of the world and the people within it.[54]

Jean-Paul Sartre had a strong idea of whom he wanted to be all the time. He refused to allow himself to be made out as a front man for ideals he did not espouse. In two occasions, Sartre refused to be recognized for his literary accomplishments.

In 1945, Sartre declined an appointment to the *French Legion d'Honneur*. In 1964, he declined a *Nobel Prize* for Literature, stating, "A writer should not allow himself to be turned into an institution."[55] Many critics were surprised to see that Sartre rejected the *Nobel* recognition.

Sartre refused to be accepted for his works. But a few observers saw this decision as an opportunity to smear Sartre. Sartre attracted more criticisms because of his refusal to accept recognitions and

---

[54] Observers argue that Sartre had a particular view of the world. As noted in the introductory section, critics viewed him as arrogant. This view probably emanated from the perception that Sartre had a condescending attitude towards those who lacked the intellectual insights to understand the world and the people within it.

[55] "Nobel Prize in Literature 1964 - Press Release," accessed August 8, 2015, http://www.nobelprize.org/nobel_prizes/literature/laureates/1964/press.html.

Chapter 2: Profession and Career Trajectory

even for his reluctance to accept accolades from his peers.

This move took critics by surprise though. The decision also sent shockwaves in the literary world. Observers were baffled about the reason Sartre rejected this prestigious recognition. Sartre provided little explanation about the reason he chose not to accept the *Nobel Prize*.

Many critics speculated wildly about the possible motives that led Sartre to make such a choice. No one knew why he declined the recognition. Sartre felt it was necessary to make it clear that he saw himself as different from other philosophers.

Sartre did not yearn for fame. He reacted to his superstar status in his own way. It could not be said that Sartre's reaction to fame was the result of his personality. It is likely that Sartre sought to avoid being in the limelight because of his strong sense of self-identity. It could also be because of Sartre's well-grounded ideology.

CHAPTER THREE

POLITICAL DISSENT

This chapter explores Sartre's role in politics. It elaborates on his military service. It examines Sartre's participation in the resistance during the German occupation. It discusses Sartre's evolution as a novelist and playwright, both during and after World War II. It recounts Sartre's theory about existentialism, including the views he espoused about freedom and self-identity. It explores the degree to which Sartre seemed entrenched in the idea that the individual has a bit of control over his need for freedom. The chapter further surveys the degree to which Jean-Paul Sartre viewed the being as he shapes his own identity in the world.

3. A Political Idealist

JEAN-PAUL SARTRE WAS a political idealist. He was often described as a political activist. In his youth, Sartre served in the military.

During World War II, Germany invaded France.[56] Sartre was drafted into the army. But he would later join the French resistance. Sartre later called for an immediate end of the German occupation.

---

[56] "Fall of France," *HISTORY*, accessed July 22, 2015, http://www.history.co.uk/study-topics/history-of-ww2/fall-of-france.

Chapter 3: A Political Idealist

Between 1939 and 1941, Sartre was active on the political front. He took part in several political efforts, which were aimed at derailing the German occupation. Sartre published many materials, which catapulted him toward literary stardom.

The next few paragraphs lay out some of Jean-Paul Sartre's political trajectories. They include his personal and intellectual efforts both during and after the war. The chapter revisits Sartre's prior works, including books and plays.

SARTRE DURING WORLD WAR II

Jean-Paul Sartre was a fierce opponent of Germany's military advancement across Europe. Around 1929, he joined the French Army. The extent of his military service is unclear. His service is often the subject of intense speculations.

The confusions about the reason Sartre joined the army is unfounded. But questions lingered on whether Sartre joined the army willingly or whether he was compelled to do so. It is worthy of note that during that period in France, most youthful men had to join the military.

During that time, joining the military was compulsory. It was described as *"Conscription,"*[57] *"Military Service,"* or « *Service Militaire.* »[58] No doubt, Sartre served in the army.[59] Although this discussion is not essential to our arguments here, it is important to avoid misrepresenting Sartre's military experience during the war.

Sartre served heroically in the military. He served about eighteen-month of military service, which he completed in 1931.[60] The mention of that experience is not to present a laudable depiction of Jean-Paul Sartre's military service records.

Serving in the army in France was a necessity to most men around the time of the German occupation. It was not out of the ordinary that a person like the young Jean-Paul would spend some time in the military during that epoch. But critics

---

[57] Philippe Catros, "Annie Crépin, Histoire de la conscription," *Annales historiques de la Révolution française*, no. 362 (December 1, 2010): 179–80.

[58] This is also known as the "Conscription" in France. This was a form of compulsory military service. This was required by the state. A portion of the French population was required to serve in the armed forces.

[59] Sartre served in the French army between 1929 and 1931.

[60] Flynn, *Sartre*.

Chapter 3: A Political Idealist

often questioned the reason Sartre joined the military. Nonetheless, Sartre had no choice but to serve in the army during that time.

While leaving that understanding aside, many believe [in a big way of course] that Sartre was drafted into the army. His military service coincided with the same period of the German invasion of the « *L'Hexagone.* » The French Army was mobilized at the outbreak of World War II.[61]

Sartre was called on duty. He served around the Eastern Front. Sartre performed the duties of a meteorologist until his capture by German forces.[62]

THE GERMAN OCCUPATION

Around 1939, the French military was mobilizing. The French army expected a possible German invasion. In anticipation of that frightened state of affairs, there was a need for soldiers.

---

[61] Jean-Paul Sartre, *Being and Nothingness*, trans. Hazel E. Barnes, Reprint edition (New York: Washington Square Press, 1993).

[62] Ann Fulton, *Apostles of Sartre: Existentialism in America, 1945-1963*, 1 edition (Evanston, Ill: Northwestern University Press, 1999).

On May 10, 1940, German forces invaded France.[63] During that time, Sartre was called to serve his country. Later the same year, the German military held Sartre captive in a prison camp.

Even as a war prisoner, Sartre was still defiant. He refused to surrender to German dominion. Sartre was insistent about the idea that the individual held his freedom at all time, even during the occupation.

The war was still growing when Sartre was released from prison. But the details are unclear about the reason he had been released. Another version of the events suggests that Sartre managed to escape on his way to Paris. To say it again, whether Sartre was a war hero is not the point I seek to make here. But what is irrefutable is that Sartre became a member of an underground group, which fought against the German invaders.

One explanation suggests that Sartre's release was because of his poor health conditions. All the same, a few critics pointed out that Sartre was

---

[63] "Fall of France."

Chapter 3: A Political Idealist

released because of drug use.[64] Several prominent voices have also risen to point out that Sartre often experimented with drugs, such as hallucinogenic.[65] Sartre admitted during an interview that he experienced with drugs while in school.[66]

It is undisputable that Jean-Paul Sartre spent several months in a German prison camp. The details are sketchy about how long he was held there. However, many believe that Sartre spent nine months as a prisoner of war. Being in prison was perhaps an intellectual blessing in disguise for the young Jean-Paul.

While in prison, Sartre developed and directed several plays for his fellow prisoners. He produced his first play; it was titled « Barionà ou Le Fils du Tonnerre » or "Barionà or the Son of Thunder." The play was successful; it marked Sartre's entry in French literature pompously.

---

[64] John Gerassi, ed., *Talking with Sartre: Conversations and Debates*, First Edition (New Haven, CT: Yale University Press, 2009).

[65] Gary Cox, *Sartre and Fiction* (A&C Black, 2009).

[66] "When Sartre Talked to Crabs (It Was Mescaline)," *The New York Times*, November 15, 2009, sec. Week in Review, http://www.nytimes.com/2009/11/15/weekinreview/15grist.html.

Sartre furthered his convictions about major philosophical principles. Sartre refined his grasp about the main ideas brought forth by the major thinkers of his era, including Heidegger. Jean-Paul Sartre also reached a broader audience. As a result, he enjoyed a more prominent status in the literary world than his predecessors could ever imagine.

Throughout the war, Sartre proved himself as a fervent patriot. He became more involved politically. On his release from prison in 1941, he joined the *Paris Resistance* movement as a journalist.[67] These efforts gained him much notoriety and an incomparable public esteem. Sartre gradually positioned himself as a reputable playwright.

A Political Activist

Despite the Nazi occupation and the brutal censorship of dissenting voices, Sartre used his literary talent to voice an uncanny opposition to the occupation. He produced an array of satirical plays,

---

[67] Sartre, *Being and Nothingness*.

Chapter 3: A Political Idealist

which aim at the German occupiers. He produced politically provocative plays, markedly a popular play known as « *Les Mouches* » *(The Flies)*, which, many viewed as a blatant stance against tyranny and a call for resistance and freedom.[68]

This play was about choice. Then, Sartre examined the effects of making correct or wrong choices.[69] This was the beginning of a lifelong examination of the being.

As a journalist, Sartre contributed to several underground newspapers.[70] He gained the reputation of a political activist. During the war, Sartre solidified his reputation as both a fervent dramatist and a prolific novelist.

Sartre was a political activist by choice. He was also a Marxist by convenience. He was an "apolitical litterateur above all else.[71]

---

[68] Sartre.

[69] W. John Campbell and Jean-Paul Sartre, *No Exit and The Flies Notes* (John Wiley & Sons, 1983).

[70] Sartre, *Being and Nothingness*.

[71] Mark Poster, *Existential Marxism in Postwar France: From Sartre to Althusser*, First Edition Thus edition (Princeton, N.J: Princeton University Press, 1976), 75; Andrew Dobson, *Jean-Paul Sartre and the Politics of Reason: A Theory of History* (Cambridge University Press, 1993), 17.

While Sartre sympathized with the *Communist Party* in France, he never embraced communism as a political ideology. Still, critics are convinced that the Sartrean approach to several philosophical issues is barely concerned with history. From this viewpoint, the Sartrean model is mainly centered on the individual.[72]

Most commentators do not deny a link between morality and politics. They also recognize Sartre's reluctance to be entangled in political issues. The problem, they argue, is that Sartre could not be a moral philosopher without interjecting himself in politics. Critics note that Sartre could never resolve the problem between ethics and politics. Other observers point out that it was ethical concerns that brought Sartre to the political arena.[73]

Sartre's political activism was, before anything else, remarkable because of his willingness to take part in public demonstrations, letter-writing campaigns, and court appearances to support those

---

[72] Andrew Dobson, *Jean-Paul Sartre and the Politics of Reason: A Theory of History* (Cambridge University Press, 1993), 17.

[73] William Leon McBride and Calvin O. Schrag, *Phenomenology in a Pluralistic Context* (SUNY Press, 1983), 31.

Chapter 3: A Political Idealist

arrested during political efforts.[74] Sartre took part in various domestic issues in France. In 1968, he was part of a student demonstration to reform the country's higher education.

Sartre was active in the international front. He was insistent about the role his country had been playing in Algeria. Sartre voiced his staunch disagreement of France's involvement in the Algerian conflict.[75] Sartre was offended by the treatments the French army had subjected the Algerian people. Sartre found it distasteful that France had become an oppressor not too long after the country was under the spell of Nazi Germany.

Sartre was shocked to see the way that the French people transformed from being the oppressed, under the German occupation, to becoming the oppressors themselves in Algeria. In 1960, he published a play « *Les Séquestrées d'Altona* » or *"The Condemned of Altona,"*[76] which depicted how the Algerian people experienced oppression. But he did so with a poignant graphic

---

[74] Patrick M. O'Neil, *Great World Writers: Twentieth Century* (Marshall Cavendish, 2004), 1338.

[75] O'Neil, 1338.

[76] O'Neil, 1338.

literary imagery. Sartre remodeled the reality of the Algerian conflict through his pen. Sartre was among the first intellectuals to call for Algeria's independence.[77]

Sartre asserted himself on other global issues, including the Vietnam War. He was critical of France's military efforts in Vietnam; he condemned the country's presence in the region. In 1965, Sartre refused to attend a series of lectures at Cornell University. He did so radically and in protest against the Vietnam War.

Sartre was outspoken in world politics. Toward the outbreak of the Cold War, Sartre was generously active politically.[78] He took a firm stance against nuclear expansion. Sartre voiced a pressing fear for nuclear annihilation.

Sartre gave lectures and speeches promoting world peace. He became a prominent personality in the world peace movement. Sartre wrote many articles on the subject. He turned himself into one of the eminent voice for the peace movement.[79]

---

[77] Sartre, *Being and Nothingness*.

[78] Robert Benewick and Philip Green, *The Routledge Dictionary of Twentieth-Century Political Thinkers* (Routledge, 2002).

[79] Benewick and Green, 281.

Chapter 3: A Political Idealist

Sartre was extraordinarily successful as a playwright. He later composed several popular and captivating plays, including « Huit-clos » (No Exit). This play is among Sartre's finest works. This particular play is produced and studied more conventionally than his other works in the discipline.[80]

Sartre produced an array of important literary works, which include « La Nausée » (Nausea) and « L'Être et le Néant » (Being and Nothingness).[81] These plays are among the major highlights of Sartre's literary career. Sartre produced several other works. Let us explore some of them in the next chapter.

---

[80] Campbell and Sartre, *No Exit and The Flies Notes*.

[81] Sartre, *Being and Nothingness*.

Chapter Four

Philosophy and other Works

Sartre compiled several publications about ethics throughout his career. This chapter examines a few of such works. The most famous contribution Sartre made to literature is by creating the journal known as "Les Temps Modernes." The chapter explores the degree to which this particular effort helped catapult Sartre to fame. The chapter also explores other facets of the works Sartre produced during and after the Second World War. It examines facets of the ideas Sartre made famous during that period.

4. Les Temps Modernes

IN 1945, SARTRE FOUNDED the prestigious journal known as « *Les Temps Modernes* » or *"Modern Times."*[82] Sartre had just turned forty years old when he created and directed the journal. Observers wondered why Sartre embarked in such an undertaken at this point in his life.[83]

---

[82] The name "Les Temps Modernes" or Modern Times is used to depict a prestigious journal founded by Jean-Paul Sartre in 1945.

[83] Ranwez, *Jean-Paul Sartre's Les Temps Modernes, a Literary History, 1945-1952.*

Chapter 4: Les Temps Modernes

Sartre was at the peak of a newly found glory in his career. He could have easily remained at the crest of the "literary intelligentsia."[84] Why did he make such a choice, observers interrogated? According to most commentators, the answer was not immediately obvious.

Sartre enjoyed the support of his friends and colleagues to catapult the journal to a status of an unparalleled literary prominence. In this effort, Simone de Beauvoir, Maurice Merleau-Ponty, and Raymond Aron, just to name a few, joined Sartre. It is worthy of note that Sartre published most of his ideas about existentialism in the journal.[85]

The journal became a reputable source for literary works by Sartre and other prominent writers, preeminently in France. The magazine was renowned internationally as a beacon for major literary works in France. The journal addressed the philosophical, the literary, and the political issues

---

[84] Ranwez.

[85] "Revue Les Temps Modernes - GALLIMARD - Site Gallimard," accessed August 8, 2015, http://www.gallimard.fr/Catalogue/GALLIMARD/Revue-Les-Temps-Modernes.

that dominated both national and world polity at the time.[86]

Towards the end of 1945, the journal, which many knew as « *La Revue,* » achieved a status of outmost prominence in the *Hexagon*.[87] The journal also helped catapulted Sartrean philosophy to an international audience.[88] Sartre was among the publishers and the editors of the journal.

By mid-1940s, Sartre had become a leading authority in philosophy and a formidable thinker in France. For more than a decade, Jean-Paul Sartre dominated French literature in various facets. He reached a similar status around the world.

SARTRE AFTER THE WAR

After World War II, Jean-Paul Sartre continued to be an inexhaustible thinker. He became a writer with innumerable talents. Since then, Sartre had a

---

[86] O'Neil, *Great World Writers*, 1338.

[87] The journal was named after a film by Charlie Chaplin titled "Modern Times" or "Les Temps Modernes in French. The film was a comedic depiction of the industrialization era. The film was released in the United States on February 25, 1936.

[88] Ibid.

Chapter 4: Les Temps Modernes

marked impact in several fields, including psychology and philosophy. Sartre produced several works that captivated readers all around the globe.

Sartre's writings transcended the way individuals could look at their selves in various environmental settings. Sartre changed the way individuals could examine their efforts within society, including within confined or controlled environments. Sartre gave ordinary peoples the tools necessary to gauge their dealings with each other.

After World War II, Sartre was on his way to literary stardom. Sartrean philosophy was viewed as a force for change. Many considered Sartre as an agent of modernity. As already recollected, his ideas resounded beyond the geographical boundaries of France and other bordering regions.

Sartre revolutionized the manner in which we could assert human behavior. Through the lens of his philosophical writings, the nature of human relations with one another became obvious to most observers. Sartre succeeded in making philosophy

"Hype" and *"Cool."* There was a point in France when everyone wanted to be an existentialist.[89]

Sartre undressed the human being. He exposed his flaws to a point where any individual could gauge himself or herself, including others in the community. Sartrean philosophy offered the possibility that we could examine the human being at a more abstract, also in a concrete, level. A Sartrean approach to phenomenology allowed valuable insights about how people could construe their role in both society and nature.

Not everyone is convinced that ontology is compatible with ethics. A few commentators argue that there is an inherent contradiction in Sartre's lecture of the being in the world. Others note that the being (or the individual) will never reach his goal in life.[90] The want to be good is impossible or else unattainable.[91] The human that Sartre projects will never come true, critics argue.[92]

---

[89] Thomas W. Busch, "The Philosophy of Jean-Paul Sartre" (Class Lecture, Villanova University, Spring 2014).

[90] McBride and Schrag, *Phenomenology in a Pluralistic Context*.

[91] McBride and Schrag.

[92] McBride and Schrag.

Chapter 4: Les Temps Modernes

FREEDOM AND SELF-IDENTITY

Sartre was committed to human freedom in his works. He argues that we could approach the individual in two ways: the *"for-itself"* and the *"in-itself."* The centerpiece of Sartrean philosophy revolves around freedom. But critics note that in *Being and Nothingness*, freedom has a neutral ontological significance.[93]

Through *"self-identity,"* Sartre sought to bridge the gap between the *"in-itself"* and the *"for-itself."* Sartrean philosophical underpinnings highlight how human beings interact in nature by their inherent capacity to be themselves in the chaos, which is nature itself. The human being enjoys certain influence on both the self and nature. But the individual may exert such an influence only through his reach for freedom.

Sartre refused to admit the slight possibility that human beings might not enjoy full control over their existence in nature. He has always been

---

[93] Richard J. Bernstein, *Praxis and Action: Contemporary Philosophies of Human Activity* (University of Pennsylvania Press, 2011).

insistent about the capacity of human beings to be free. Sartre believes that destiny is an elusive idea. From the Sartrean viewpoint, there is no such a thing in nature. Instead, the being is in charge of his reality within the natural [social] environment.

Sartre typifies that the individual settles his own destiny. By it, each individual can forge a particular assessment of the extent of destiny within the environment in which he grows. The being builds his destiny in the world. The being is free to engage nature or society as he sees fit.

Sartre's major theoretical approach centers on the notion that human beings are intrinsically free. For Sartre, human freedom is not just physical. The freedom itself is also abstract. The individual can construe his freedom from nature and from other environments. The being may experience freedom in various settings at will.

CONDEMNED TO BE FREE

Sartre argues that the individual is condemned to be free. Sartre further recognizes that the being may also ignore his freedom. The Sartrean approach to human ontology assumes that human beings can accept or reject their freedom within nature or society.

Sartre intimates that the individual controls his fate in nature. Only he (for example, the individual or the being) could restrict his freedom by refusing to recognize him (self) within nature. When the individual refuses to accept the reality within his environment, he is said to be in *bad faith* (Mauvaise foi), Sartre argues.

The term *bad faith* is among the highlights of existentialism. This is the heart of the Sartrean approach to philosophy, I would contend. At some point, this term was popular in France. Unabridged, it reached similar popularity around the world. The term became a way to qualify [or to quantify] human conducts in their intransigence in nature or within society.

We could not speak of a Sartrean philosophy today without evoking the doctrine of bad faith. We could understand this idea as the physical expression of the individual capacity to construe his reality. This is the essence of a Sartrean approach to freedom.

The notion of *bad faith* is the foundation of the Sartrean theory about existentialism. Chapter 10 discusses this Sartrean label in depth. The next section summarizes the debate; it also outlines the method I used in the book.[94]

The next few chapters delve deeper in the debate, although they do so in a nutshell. They explore the intricate nature of Jean-Paul Sartre's writings about ethics.[95] From this point forward, the focus of our discussions will examine the point at which Sartre deserves credits for his works about morality.

---

[94] The methodology used in the book is based on a content analysis design. This approach is based on the method of exploring and analyzing words or phrases within a particular set of documents or text. In this instance, I explored the literature about Jean-Paul Sartre. I narrowed my examination on the nature or the extent of Sartrean ethics.

[95] This approach is mostly centered on a qualitative examination of the information presented in the text. The current inquiry is not the product of a formal examination of the available information on the subject. The information outlined here was not retrieved or evaluated from an academic standpoint. The organization of the book itself is based on a methodic approach the subject. The goal was to delineate meanings and links among words and arguments that are often levied against Sartre. There was no coding or the creation of specific categories to examine the question posed in the text.

Chapter 4: Les Temps Modernes

SECTION 2

SARTREAN MORAL IDENTITY

This section examines the essence of the term *"Ethics."* It explores the authenticity argument. It explains why Sartrean ethics matters. It examines the extent to which Sartre has an identity in moral philosophy. It explores whether we could consider Sartre as the owner of his views about morality. It recounts the crux of the debate.

Chapter Five

Examining the Term "Ethics"

This chapter examines the etymology of the term ethics. It elaborates on the notion of Sartrean ethics. It examines the features of the term, including Metaethics, Applied Ethics, and Normative Ethics. The chapter explores the difference between *"Ethics"* and *"Morality."* It examines four popular ethical models. They include the *"Ethics of Profession,"* the *"Ethics of Care,"* the *"Ethics of Justice,"* and the *"Ethics of Critique."*

5. What is Ethics?

THE ESSENCE OF THE ARGUMENTS echoed here projects that we could examine ethics and ontology on a similar plane. To appreciate the soul of Sartrean ethics, we might have to examine facets of Sartre's major ideas about human ontology. We might also have to examine the works of popular scholars, many of whom disentangled the degree to which Sartre deserves recognition as a philosopher.

The next few sections are informative. But the focus is on understandings that support Sartrean ethics. The goal is to explore works that both

Chapter 5. What is Ethics?

admirers and dissenters recognized as Sartre's real contribution in ethical writings.

Sartrean ethics is not without a theoretical foundation. I refute the major claims echoed in the literature. Still, the primary aim is to examine the topic without detour.

My arguments do not clarify the reasons Sartre's works receive little or no appreciation in most literary circles. I do not address the motives that opponents may have to rebuff Sartre's role in ethics. Granted, I am not concerned with the reason critics often treated Sartre's works in the field to a lesser esteem. Anyway, I seek to interject a neutral approach in the conversation.

Let me elaborate on what I mean by the term *"Sartrean Ethics."* What does the terms *"Sartrean"* and *"ethics"* stand for? What frames the idea known as *"Moral Philosophy?"* The same, what are the characteristics of a *"Moral Philosopher?"*

All these are valid questions. I do not address them in depth here. My priority is to explain the essence of a Sartrean approach to ethics. It is not to discuss the term ethics itself.

The present volume could not explain all the underpinnings of Sartrean ethics. In deciphering

Sartre's role in moral philosophy, the goal is to find answers. It is not to add to the confusion in the debate.

I do not offer this work as the sole defense of Sartrean ethics. There is more to the issues. But this work is a way to acknowledge the role Sartre played in setting up the foundation of his moral thoughts.

As you delve in the manuscript, you will uncover more about the issues. Sartrean ethics exists, although it might be embryonic. It is best to acknowledge this ethics rather than dismissing it altogether.

Scholars of all creeds and literary expertise struggled to pinpoint the nature of Sartrean ethics. Few inquirers have been able to decipher that ethics. There is little agreement about the extent of Sartre's contribution to the field. But that ethics is not as elusive as many purport it to be.

Etymology of the Term Ethics

Ethics is an elastic terminology; it stands for notions of virtue or moral virtue. In his famous

Chapter 5. What is Ethics?

1899 book titled *"The School and Society,"* John Dewey suggests that ethics is a scientific terminology, which focuses on human conduct, scilicet notions of *right* and *wrong*, or *good* and *bad*.[96] The term could be approached from several angles.

Although the term has various practical uses or understandings, it is often approached as a branch of moral philosophy. Ethics is an important part of various philosophical principles. I use the term under the penumbra of moral philosophy or philosophy in general.

The link I propose between ontology and ethics is not that obscure. It is plain in the arguments presented in this literature. There is a link between Sartre's approaches to human conduct, ethics, and phenomenology. Ethics is an important part in Sartrean philosophy. Grasping the roots of the term might be crucial in helping us unlock the nature or the fullness of the Sartrean approach.

Ethical ideas are often deciphered in notions about morality. Ethics can be understood within the context of moral values and moral duties. The

---

[96] John Dewey, *The Child and the Curriculum* (Martino Fine Books, 2011). The original book was published under the title "The School and Society."

term also includes notions of human freedom and choice, human flourishing, human relations, excellence and merit, and radical critiques.[97]

Interpretations dealing with ethics are based on three features: *Metaethics*, *Applied Ethics*, and *Normative Ethics*.[98] There is a relation between ethics and human ontology. That tie unquestionably settles a link between morality and existentialism. Let us assess these ethical notions in depth.

THE FEATURES OF ETHICS

The term *Metaethics* can be understood as the study of the foundations of morality or the nature of moral debate.[99] This understanding is concerned with moral facts, moral language, and moral judgments. This approach to morality deals with notions of virtue, namely persuasions that are relevant to what is true or false. It deals with

---

[97] Stephen Darwall, *Philosophical Ethics* (Westview Press, 1998).

[98] James Fieser, "Ethics | Internet Encyclopedia of Philosophy," accessed August 7, 2015, http://www.iep.utm.edu/ethics/.

[99] "Metaethics | Define Metaethics at Dictionary.com," accessed August 7, 2015, http://dictionary.reference.com/browse/metaethics.

Chapter 5. What is Ethics?

notions applying to subjectivity and objectivity, including insights about morality.

Applied ethics, on the other hand, is concerned with the practical facets of moral judgments. As the name suggests, this is a more hands-on perspective to ethical realities. This approach is concerned with politics, economics, and other societal realities.

This model to ethics is often relegated to professional organizations. Applied ethics is, in general terms, concerned with setting up philosophical arguments tailored to tackle a particular organizational problem.[100] This specific branch of ethics is dedicated to grasping moral problems. Applied ethics encompass policies in personal life, professions, technology, and government.[101]

Normative ethics is geared towards inferences describing moral principles. This approach is based on fixed norms of conducts. Normative ethics highlights the nature of moral virtue.

---

[100] James R. Rest and Darcia Narvez, Moral Development in the Professions: Psychology and Applied Ethics (Psychology Press, 1994).

[101] Thomas Søbirk Petersen et al., "Applied Ethics," May 10, 2010, http://www.oxfordbibliographies.com/display/id/obo-9780195396577-0006.

From this approach, ideas about normative ethics address issues that are relevant to the sudden inclination of taking actions (for example, the greater good) that would benefit the greatest number. This understanding is better left to journalists, politicians, and preachers.[102]

EXAMINING APPROACHES

Other approaches to the term ethics are also worth revisiting here. We could understand this term from a legal lens. Id est, we could examine the term ethics as a larger societal issue. Ethics is the affairs of the laws of society and the extent to which people uphold them.[103]

These approaches do not sketch the true meaning of the term. There is more to the idea itself than just referring to it as notions of *right* and *wrong*. Etymologically speaking, the term *"Ethics"*

---

[102] Leonard Wayne Sumner, "Normative Ethics and Metaethics," *Ethics* 77, no. 2 (January 1, 1967): 95–106.

[103] Manuel Velasquez et al., "What Is Ethics?," Fall 1987, http://www.scu.edu/ethics/practicing/decision/whatisethics.html.

Chapter 5. What is Ethics?

refers to *habitudes* and *customs*. Those two connotations often intertwine with human conducts. Understandings addressing ethical problems cannot be dissociated with beliefs about human ontology.

The term ethics originated from an ancient Greek *"Vocable."* The Greek word for it is *"Ethikos,"* which arises from another Greek word known as *"Ethos."* This term also suggests the existence of certain customs or uses. The customs must exist in relation (or in reference) to setting up a particular standard. With philosophy, the term is more complex; it can only be appreciated narrowly.[104]

PARADIGMS OF ETHICS AND MORALITY

What is ethics? Is there a clear demarcation between ethics and morality? Is there a clear divide between ethical systems of belief and philosophical notions about those beliefs? Answering these questions may demand a thorough investigation

---

[104] The term Micro level is used to illustrate the study of the individual, not an entire community. In philosophy, ethics is relegated to individual scrutiny.

about the term ethics. For brevity, however, I will only examine the term superficially here.

I sought to explain in the previous section that ethical notions are often interlocked with notions about moral philosophy. I use both terms interchangeably in this work.[105] We could approach the term "ethics" from various perspectives.

We could understand ethics from four models. They are as follows: *Profession, Justice, Care,* and *Critique*. Let us explore them in greater length.

We could approach understandings about ethical issues from a professional lens. This examination of the idea has led to the popular term known as *"Professional Ethics"* or the *"Ethics of Profession."* From this angle, ethics is best examined in a particular profession or trade.

We could appreciate the term from the lens of caring. This ethics is habitually described as the *"Ethics of Care."*[106] The individual develops a caring attitude. He approaches issues from a utilitarian

---

[105] In this book, I use the terms "ethics" and "moral philosophy" interchangeably.

[106] Carol Gilligan, *In a Different Voice: Psychological Theory and Women's Development* (Cambridge, Mass: Harvard University Press, 1998).

Chapter 5. What is Ethics?

perspective. In the ethics of care, there is a nurturing connection among individuals.

The term is often broached within the lens of justice. Ideas about rights and laws play an important role in ethical issues. This approach to ethics draws from the works of Thomas Hobbes and Emmanuel Kant. But other philosophers, including Jean-Jacques Rousseau, Georg Wilhelm Friedrich Hegel, John Dewey, and Karl Marx, played a big role in developing this ethical approach. This intellectual perspective about the extent of morality is broadly known as the *"Ethics of Justice."*

We could understand ethics as a critique. However, the focus here is on the larger societal issues that permeate human relations. We could examine social problems inquisitively. This outlook about the term is comprehensively branded as the *"Ethics of Critique."* This approach is also grounded in a Kantian philosophical model.

Sartrean ethics is more complex and has many layers than the approaches (for example, justice, care, profession, and critique). Assessing that ethics from the models noted earlier could be too broad.

Explanations might not accurately help us answer the questions posed earlier.

To reiterate, this publication is limited to the writings of Jean-Paul Sartre. I do not delve in questions about ethics globally. But what is Sartrean ethics? What are the characteristics of that ethical approach? Let us explore.

THE TERM SARTREAN ETHICS

In the preceding paragraphs, I sought to examine the term ethics. What is the difference between ethics *in general* and ethics from *a Sartrean lens*? Let us examine this term a little bit further to understand how it applies to Jean-Paul Sartre.

Understandings about the term ethics could be inaccurate. They could lead to uncertainties. The term ethics is broad. It includes an array of ideas.

Depending on how we approach the term itself, we could narrow it down to a specific instance or a particular subject. Because of the nature of the term, its meanings often vary. This is markedly so, I would say, in certain fields of study.

Chapter 5. What is Ethics?

Moral philosophy falls within the tradition of abstract theory. As such, interpretations about the term could be strikingly subjective. Ethical explanations are often the subject of intense debates.

The term *"Sartrean Ethics"* has a much narrower interpretation. Its meaning could be hard to decipher. This term is routinely associated with Jean-Paul Sartre, the man.

Sartrean ethics is construed at an individualistic level. Sartre himself embodies that ethical ideal. From this perspective, this notion is mostly based on Sartre's own views about human conducts within their environment.

The term *"Sartrean"* or « *Sartrien/Sartrienne* » (in French Literature) is a philosophical connotation, which notes Jean-Paul Sartre's own theory about certain moral issues. We could approach ethics by examining the moral principles that guide human conducts in the world. We could understand Sartrean ethics as the manner in which Sartre himself examined individual conducts within the environment, including in the natural milieu or in a social milieu.

This treatment to ethical issues does not encompass works produced by other philosophers. When I speak of the ethics of Jean-Paul Sartre, I refer to the works Sartre published or produced in the moral philosophy.[107] I appraised whether he had developed a true ethics throughout his career.

---

[107] As I will discuss further, there is a clear distinction between works produced and works published. Sartre produced all his works. In chapter 5, I talk about the authenticity or the ownership of Sartre's works. The distinction I am trying to establish here centers on the fact that Sartre did not publish all his works himself.

As I point out in Sartre's literary imprint, Sartre produced over 45 books. Eight of them had been published posthumously. Critics regard these works as different in literary valor; this is at least the case when it comes to ethics.

Chapter 5. What is Ethics?

Chapter Six

An Authentic Ethics

This chapter explores the weight of Sartrean philosophy with ethics. It delves into the reason examining that ethics is important. The chapter recounts the presumption that Sartre has preserved a genuine voice in moral philosophy. The chapter offers a novel approach to examine Sartre and his major literary exploits. It also discusses the arguments offered in favor and against the idea that Sartrean philosophy has an ethical dimension.

6. The Authenticity Approach

WE COULD UNDERSTAND Sartrean ethics as an accurate examination of the study of morality. While the usefulness of this approach is contentious, my goal is to incite a positive attitude in the literature. I also hope this discussion will allow those who have had little or no exposure to the topic grasp the seriousness of the current literary debate. I will do my best to sketch out Sartre's relevance in ethics as concisely as possible.

Chapter 6. The Authenticity Approach

I will examine published works about Sartrean ethics, including some works he published posthumously. The nature of my discussion will center on the works he tailored respectively for ethics. I will argue that his scheme to testing important ethical issues is genuine.

Most of the works Sartre produced, which are referenced from one end to the other in this volume, are not recent. Many of them had been written between the 1940s and the 1960s. However, most of those works had only been uncovered or released to the public within the last few decades. These works include a plethora of materials, which Sartre prepared for a series of lectures he gave or intended to give in various countries, which include higher educational institutions in the United States.[108]

In these writings, Sartre seemed confident about the role of ethics in fermenting human conducts. He sounded firm about the link that exists between morality and freedom. This proves that Sartre understood the purposive role ethical notions play in allowing individuals to construe

---

[108] Johnson, *Sartrean Ethics*.

their duties or their responsibilities within their environment.

Sartre highlighted a genuine ethical segment in his publications. Based on the noted viewpoint (perhaps contrary to popular assumptions), a Sartrean ethics exists. Sartre deserves some merits for his intellectual role in the field. I argue that this ethics is worthy of proper recognitions.

The tendency in various scholarly circles is to reject Sartre's role in ethics altogether. Sartre produced no materials that plainly underlined broader ethical issues, they say. But this view is not accurate. Let me explain why.

It is indisputable that Sartre contributed to moral philosophy. Dismissing the valor of his publications in the domain of ethics would not advance his literary legacy. Rebuking his works would not be fair to his efforts as a writer.

Many sought to rebuke Sartre. Embracing such a position against him could only undermine his intellectual worth. This approach to the works Sartre produced in the domain could hurt his legacy.

Chapter 6. The Authenticity Approach

WHY EXAMINING SARTREAN ETHICS?

You might ask why writing a book about Jean-Paul Sartre. So much has been written or said about this prominent philosopher. Why examining his writings in the domain of ethics in particular, why now? My answer would be, why not. Let me further explain the reason I would answer these questions that way.

Although Sartrean philosophy is well studied, a Sartrean approach to moral philosophy is still clouded with inaccurate assumptions about the man and his intellectual merit in the field. There is no dearth of discussions about Sartrean philosophy. There is no lack of rebuttals about the extent of his thoughts about morality.

Criticisms abound from different literary circles. To this degree, it is always relevant to examine misguided condemnations against Sartre. My examination will center on such contentions.

Criticisms against Sartre have no boundaries. Even facets of Sartre's personal life have often been the subjects of intense scrutiny. More often than not, Sartre's most intimate secrets have been discussed with little or no regards for his privacy. A decade-old publication by Hazel Rowley depicts a morally bankrupt Sartre.[109] The publication was popular during the time of its early release.

In her acclaimed book, *Tête-à-Tête* (2005), Rowley paints Sartre as a passionate lover, a man with an incommensurable appetite for depravity or debauchery almost for adolescent girls.[110] Rowley came close of classifying Sartre as a pedophile. In the same vein, the author fell short of calling Beauvoir a promoter of Sartre's romantic escapades or an instigator of Sartre's sexual leanings.

Other critics were cruder in their reaction to the revelations Rowley publicized. Todd McEwen and Lucy Ellmann, for instance, made little denial in their description of the pair. They referred to Sartre as a "classic philanderer straight out of Moliere."[111]

As for Beauvoir, these critics lambasted her complaisance and her make-belief magnanimity in

---

[109] The book was published in 2005 in French. The English translation was published in 2006 by Harper Collins.

[110] Rowley, *Tete-a-Tete*.

[111] Todd McEwen and Lucy Ellmann, "Damp Squibs," *The Guardian*, January 14, 2006, sec. Books, http://www.theguardian.com/books/2006/jan/14/highereducation.biography.

Chapter 6. The Authenticity Approach

these existentialists' project to deceive the public about their moral correctness. Such duplicity, many commentators resounded, does not make Beauvoir a victim of Sartre's grip. But it does make her an important Sartre's acolyte, which also makes her less important on the intellectual plane.

Rowley highlighted a side of Jean-Paul Sartre, which, if it existed, few people would recognize or were aware of its extent. That is not all; in the publication, the author revealed intimate facets of the romantic liaison, which Sartre supposedly entertained with Beauvoir.[112]

The unflattering depictions of these prominent representatives of existentialism could fuel spurn against them. Such depictions could also help cast doubts about their moral authority, which, in turn, might also raise more questions about the nature of Sartrean philosophy or even the degree to which Sartrean ethics is important. I refute these types of works; they are akin to character assassinations.

What predominately motivates criticisms against Jean-Paul Sartre? A succinct answer to this

---

[112] Rowley claimed that most of the works included in the book came from letter that Beauvoir wrote or believed to have written about her life and the life of Jean-Paul Sartre.

question is not always obvious. Sartre's moral thoughts are often rebuked. A genuine understanding about his contributions to the field remains dubious.

At this point, it is not clear whether disagreements are based on personal views or whether they are motivated by preconceived notions about Sartre himself. The latter possibility is more likely. It is also unclear whether the claims levied in the literature are well thought-out.

This is besides the point I seek to explain here. My goal is simplistic. There is a need to explore, as convincingly as possible, the nature, or the relevance, of the many objections against Sartre's formula to examining ethical issues.

I am not sure whether a clear link exists between Sartre's personal views about morality and his procedure to examine ethics. It could be irrelevant on whether Sartre was a puritan or whether he was morally depraved. But critics do not make out such a difference. Still, it is important to draw a clear divide between Sartre's disposition to examining morality and the depth of his moral sanctity.

Chapter 6. The Authenticity Approach

Jean-Paul Sartre was not a saint. I am not concerned with his personal choices or his lifestyle. Rather, I am interested with his intellectual contributions to philosophy, for example ethics.

Sartre enjoyed an unparalleled mastery of certain abstract ideas. Ethics, I would argue, was one of them. In his major works, he hinted that mastery of ethical issues rather eloquently. From that understanding, I am confident that most criticisms against his approach to morality are in error.

I am convinced (beyond the shadow of a doubt) that Sartre outlines reasonable arguments to support his ethical concerns. He did so in most of his major philosophical works (for example, works published both while alive and postmortem). Sartre's intrepidity is no match for temerarious critics.

Often, objections come from all angles and from many levels of expertise. We could understand their goals as disorienting. It is not always clear what critics want when they criticize Sartre.

For many observers, Sartrean ethics is non-existent. Is there any truth to that viewpoint? I would say no. You could rebuke my answer; you could consider it subjective. I will try to explore the literature with an unprejudiced mind set. Perhaps in doing so, we might be able to find a way to mitigate views against Sartre as objectively as possible.

OWNERSHIP OF HIS ETHICS

Jean-Paul Sartre is the sole owner of his moral thoughts. His deliberations about morality are undoubtedly intertwined with facets of his approach to phenomenology. This show that Sartre's philosophical ideals had not been supplemented or adjusted by other writers. Sartre's ethical concerns remained as pristine as he sought to utter them to us.

Sartre was not drawn to ethics by accident. He had an interest in deciphering human conducts in the world. We could regard that interest as the source of his moral thoughts.

Sartre understood the ramifications of ethical realities in human freedom. How could the being be free without first understanding the need for

Chapter 6. The Authenticity Approach

such freedom? To answer this question, let us examine how Sartre imagined human freedom.

Understandings about freedom require a good grasp of complex philosophical principles. It is important to appreciate the intricacies of the conditions that might hamper an individual to earn freedom. From a Sartrean instrumentation of the term itself, freedom is, at least at first, an objective appreciation of a person's reality. But such freedom is also quantifiable.

To be free is to be aware of the possibility of not being free. Freedom is the absence of constraints, might they be mental, physical, or psychological. The being cannot be free or he cannot make out his freedom unless he can set up what that freedom would or should look like. That understanding, in turn, would promote this freedom. Thus, any "examination" of the being is also an exploration of morality.

Moreover, it could be said that any approach to human ontology involves a scrutiny of human ethics. Sartre could not avoid [or ignore] the ethical ramifications of the ideas he incited in his writings. Ethics is inherent in Sartrean philosophy, although it has a subtle presence in many facets.

Ben Wood Johnson

Sartre enjoyed exploring ethical issues. His scrutiny of the being [or his assessment] of the individual was unique. To this degree, we could consider his examination of human ontology as genuine. This view, if proven true, would show that Sartre had a deeper commitment to moral philosophy than he had been previously credited.

Sartrean ethics is valid. Sartre's works, including items he published or the works published on his behalf, had not been merged with the works of other philosophers or scholars. These works frame Sartre's intellectual property and are, plainly, part of his literary legacy. Inasmuch, Sartre remains the sole owner of his ethics, even beyond the grave.

A NEUTRAL APPROACH

We could interpret the moral philosophy of Jean-Paul Sartre anyway we want. Indeed, there is little or no uniformity in the ideas that Sartre proposed in his writings. But I will go to the limit to underline the need to examine Sartrean ethics comprehensively. This goal is achievable so long as

Chapter 6. The Authenticity Approach

the focus of this inquiry is on the extent of Sartre's examination of human ontology.

An all-inclusive approach may reveal that Sartre was actively seeking to set up an ethical part in his works. Because Sartre was not a prolific writer does not disclose much about his intellectual merit or his scholarly capacities. This reality does not disqualify him as an important player in moral philosophy either.

There is an ethical dimension in every facet of human freedom. That view is based on the Sartrean approach to human ontology. One could say that a person could not be free unless he deprives freedom from someone else. But the nature of that depravation could only be examined on the ethical realm. Let us explore this idea further.

From a Sartrean perspective, freedom is about the one who lacks it; it is also conditioned by the one who dispenses it. Freedom is not intimately innate. Freedom is an earned state of being within the natural; it is that way as well within a particular social setting.

The search for freedom must be based on certain pre-established norms and values. Any step toward freedom must also be with ethical concerns.

Whatever the individual does, or whatever he prevents the self from doing, is intrinsically ethical.

Similar understandings are also changed and openly loud throughout Sartre's major works. In *Being and Nothingness*, Sartre argues that "Existential psychoanalysis is going to reveal to man the real goal of his pursuit, which is being as a synthetic fusion of the in-itself with the for-itself; existential psychoanalysis is going to acquaint man with his passion."[113] Thus, it might be impossible to appreciate the being without grasping his moral values. Ethics offer a much-needed insight into the psychoanalysis of individual conducts.

For most observers, the proposed link between ethics and individual conducts is precisely the reason it is necessary to criticize Jean-Paul Sartre. Critics are quick to point out that Sartre failed to sketch the extent of freedom with ethics. Considering that we could link ethical notions with several notions about individual freedom, misjudging human ethics could also affect our understandings of the freedom that Sartre meant in his writings.

---

[113] Sartre, *Being and Nothingness*, 797.

Chapter 6. The Authenticity Approach

Critics note that ethics is one of those disciplines that Sartre recognized that he did not integrate fully in his works. Nonetheless, Sartre never poised himself as an expert in the field. We could relegate this view to debating the semantics of the term "expert." Discovering who is or who should be an expert is not set in stone. But as explained in previous sections, Sartre seemingly considered himself a moral philosopher.

Whether Sartre saw himself as an expert in the field is an original question, which we could decipher separately. We could make the argument that, whether we should consider Sartre as an expert in ethical writings is irrelevant to settle his crowning intellectual worth or the extent of his contribution to the ethical discipline. We could relegate this to a subjective approach. But that astuteness is not relevant here.

In human ontology, Sartre struggled to balance between the human project and ethics. This struggle was poignant in the notion of freedom. Sartre accepted that he was uncertain whether ethics incited freedom or whether the opposite is also true. He pondered about the extent of freedom without the role of ethics.

Sartre inquired in *Being and Nothingness* whether freedom would "be reapprehended from behind by the value which it wishes to contemplate."[114] Sartre reflected on whether the presence of freedom would "by the very fact that it apprehends itself as a freedom in relation to itself, be able to put an end to the reign of this value."[115]

Sartre examined the role individual values or social norms might play in human conducts. But he came short from solving this enigma. We could find answers "on the ethical plane," Sartre noted.[116]

Sartre promised to dedicate his future works to this inquiry.[117] I explained in other works (for example, the text titled Sartrean Ethics) — rather convincingly, I would say — the reason Sartre failed to honor this promise.[118] But this view is among the distinct types of rejections that are often offered in the literature against Sartre. Such criticisms are too

---

[114] Sartre, 797.

[115] Sartre, 798.

[116] Sartre, 798.

[117] Sartre, 798.

[118] Please see the title Sartrean Ethics to learn more about the reason Sartre did not honor his promise to dedicate a project about ethics, at least while alive. Johnson, *Sartrean Ethics*.

Chapter 6. The Authenticity Approach

harsh towards the Sartrean literary contribution to moral philosophy. The grounds for most rebuttals against Sartrean ethics are often misguided. They come from mistaken assumptions about the works published on Sartre's behalf posthumously.

In the mentioned book, I pointed out that Sartre did not publish any completed works about ethics. At least, he did not do so during his lifetime. These circumstantialities should not be reason enough to devalue the works Sartre compiled about ethics, though he did not publish them personally.

In sum, critics pointed out that Sartre's approach to morality is ambiguous and complicated. In that, nothing is clear about the point of origin of this ethics. His ideas are abstract and rambling, commentators contended. Critics also argue that Sartre does not consider larger social constraints in the human project.

I am not convinced that the previous arguments capture the caliber of Sartrean ethics. I am doubtful of the underlining premise here. I question the veracity of arguments that are based on the assumption that Sartre has little or no intellectual merit in ethics. Anyway, this idea is worthy of further scrutiny. Let me do so in the next chapter.

Chapter Seven

Sartre: The Moral Philosopher

This chapter assesses important characteristics of Jean-Paul Sartre as a major thinker. It explores his skills and literary contributions to examine the being, uniquely within a particular social setting or a community. The chapter describes the idea known as human ontology. It summarizes the role of individual freedom in relations to morality. The chapter sets the tone for understanding Sartre's approach to moral values.

7. A Major Thinker

JEAN-PAUL SARTRE WAS an existentialist in all angles or by any definition. In a manner consistent to his philosophy, Sartre lived his life like a free spirit. Despite pervasive inquiries [or arguments to the contrary], he died in the same way. Sartre was a true existentialist.

Sartre sought to deny both God and nature a prominent place in his life. For him, existence paves the ways for essence. Thus, for Sartre existence is before essence.

Chapter 7. A Major Thinker

Sartre argues that the being does not hold a human nature. The being exists anterior to his nature. The being cannot be defined by any idea grounded in understandings about nature. The being exists above all else. He burst out of the world and defines himself afterwards, Sartre notes.

Jean-Paul Sartre was a major theorist. His insights helped human beings understand their reality in ways never thought possible. Via his theory about human existence, in this case, *Existentialism*, Sartre gave the individual an unprecedented access to his most intimate secrets. Because of the ideas recounted in Sartre's theoretical approach, the being can examine his existence with ease.[119]

The Sartrean approach to phenomenology helped the human species rise above its ontological limits. Human beings can now reach beyond their daily rituals. They are also able, if so wished, to make sense of it all, within their environment (for example, their social and natural environments).

---

[119] Throughout this book, I use the terms being and individual interchangeably. I also use the term person to depict a being, an individual, or a human entity.

Ontologically speaking, a person could attach meanings to his life. He could also leap (that is, back and forth) to the present and to the past. The individual has the impression that he could shape his world at will.

The being could decipher the meaning of any previous experience. He could set up the past, present, and future conducts. Holding that power over one-self and over others would have enormous responsibilities. Such responsibilities could also be, at least in substance, ethical at their core. Sartre recognized the extent of that ethical inherency in his writings.

An Introspective Tool

Thanks to Sartrean philosophy, the human being has a better sense of his existence in the world. The being can entrench himself in his reality like never before. He has a sense of his capacity to envisage the reality of others in a pivotal ontological sense.

Sartre granted the being the introspective tool(s) necessary to examine his actions within the environment. The being has reasons to be

Chapter 7. A Major Thinker

concerned about the way he interacts with others. He has the means to do something about those concerns. No question about it; Sartre helped transcend popular understandings about the way human beings conduct themselves in the world.

This splendid depiction of Sartrean philosophy, the Sartrean approach to ethics, is not shared in the literature. Critics pointed out many flaws in Sartre's approach. The biggest objection raised within the literature is related to what many analysts refer as *the imperfect nature* of Jean-Paul Sartre's writings on ethics.

The belief often noted by most critics is that Sartrean philosophy is empty of an ethical part. Many commentators admit that Sartre provided some hints about his stance on ethics. They also propose that Sartre fell short of outlining what those concerns are and how to best approach them. In it lives the essence of the debate.

Commentators often echo that a Sartrean ethics is an illusion. They prodigiously argue that Sartre did not play a major role in this discipline. As far as this understanding is adopted by most observers, no argument shall be had apropos the intellectual merit of that ethics.

The previous disagreement is chronologically inaccurate. It is factually inaccurate as well. This view could misinform those who have had little or no acquaintance to Sartre's works.

Sartre compiled several works in ethics. His approach to moral philosophy is well documented.[120] Yet, critics contend that this ethics is elusive. Why is there such ingenuity in the debate about Sartrean ethics?

In *Being and Nothingness*, Sartre recognizes the unavoidable failure of all human projects.[121] Critics contend that the ethics Sartre meant—and that the being must strive to achieve at all time—is unattainable. Istvan Meszaros, for instance, notes that Sartrean ethics offers no road for realizing that ethics.

---

[120] Thomas Anderson documents the evolution of Sartrean ethics in the book titled: Sartre's Two Ethics: Thomas C. Anderson, *Sartre's Two Ethics: From Authenticity to Integral Humanity* (Chicago, Ill: Open Court Publishing Company, 1993). Anderson argues that he was tired of relying on others' works in order to examine the nature of Sartrean ethics. Since a significant amount of Sartre's own works on the subject had been made available, it was time for him to rely solely on what Sartre had chronicled about his moral thoughts.

[121] McBride and Schrag, *Phenomenology in a Pluralistic Context*, 6.

Chapter 7. A Major Thinker

Meszaros outlines what he notes as "The dilemma of Sartrean ethics." The Sartrean approach to ethics is a chimerical effort. From Meszaros' vantage point, "ethics is for us inevitable and at the same time impossible."[122]

Despite contentions to the contrary, Thomas Anderson notes that every facet of Sartrean ethics, chiefly his early ethics, is decipherable, on a large scale through the notebooks he compiled, which served as the foundation for the book known as « *Cahiers pour une morale* » or "*Notebooks for an Ethics.*" Anderson writes:

"While these six hundred pages of notes do not constitute a completed text and comprise only about one-fifth of a larger collection which was lost, they still furnish great deal of insight into the ethics Sartre was developing complementary to, and grounded in, his early ontology."[123]

This ethics could be appreciated through the materials Sartre compiled, which his adoptive

---

[122] Istvan Meszaros, *The Work of Sartre* (New York: Monthly Review Press, 2012), 261.

[123] Thomas C. Anderson, "Sartre's Early Ethics and the Ontology of Being Ad Nothingness," in *Sartre Alive* (Detroit: Wayne State University Press, 1991), 184.

daughter, finally, made available on his behalf. Most of the materials Sartre produced include manuscripts and other transcripts, which he compiled sometimes around 1964 and 1965. It is now known that Sartre's works in the domain date all the way back to the late 1930s and even the early 1940s.[124]

Critics contend these works have no intellectual worth, at least to set up the theoretical underpinnings of an ethics. From their vantage point, such works deserve to be ignored. I disagree with that viewpoint. Let me explain why.

Sartre has an important intellectual merit in moral philosophy. I seek to redirect the debate toward a lesser hostile interpretation of the role Sartre might have played in setting up his ethical ideals. The arguments interjected here should encourage critics to reconsider their article of faith about the caliber of Jean-Paul Sartre in the ethical discipline.

Sartre's writings are worthy of a positive intellectual scrutiny.[125] The views I project here do

---

[124] Johnson, *Sartrean Ethics*.

[125] Here, I use the terms "Sartrean ethics" and "Sartrean writings" interchangeably.

Chapter 7. A Major Thinker

not align with popular viewpoints. Sartre developed a true ethics throughout his literary career. Ignoring that ethics could amount to an intellectual injustice. Let us examine the origins of that ethics further.

HUMAN ONTOLOGY AND ETHICS

There is an undeniable link between the study of human ontology and the study of human ethics. As Elkaïm-Sartre notes, while many know Sartre for his works about phenomenology, he had been much engaged in ethics since 1939.[126] To this degree, it might be difficult to decipher the extent of human ontology without meddling in Sartre's ideas about ethics.

The preceding contention suggests that Sartre perhaps wrote his first lines about his moral thoughts around that time. Elkaïm-Sartre revealed that Sartre's writings about ethics, singularly in his book « *Cahiers pour une morale,* » precede his works in *"Being and Nothingness."* Thus, Sartre was a

---

[126] Jean Paul Sartre, *Cahiers pour une morale* (Paris: Gallimard, 1983).

moral philosopher before he evolved into an existentialist, assuming that the two ideas are, by their own nature, different.

What could explain the reason Jean-Paul Sartre thought it might be necessary to dedicate his future works to ethics? Would not it be easier for him to integrate his ethical ideals in his collections about human ontology? Could not he dedicate a book chapter to ethics? I am not sure that anyone other than Sartre could answer this question.

One could assume that Sartre sought to approach the being on the ethical plane before he settled for examining the being on the ontological plane. Perhaps Sartre sought to dissect human ontology, while neglecting the aptness of ethics. Perhaps Sartre did not ignore the role of ethics in his examination of the being.

Sartre was aware of the effects of morality or moral values on human conducts, although he was uncertain whether such moral concerns would incite human conducts or vice versa. In *Being and Nothingness*, for instance, Sartre pointed out that ontology could not develop its own ethical features. Yet, his ideas about that ontology role as a launch pad for his ethical concerns. Sartre

Chapter 7. A Major Thinker

understood that examining human ontology could be a precondition to grasping important ethical ramifications to understanding the human condition.

Ethical issues are not always obvious within the existentialist model. Within that context, it is important to make out the role ethics may play in construing individual conducts. Any approach to ontology could be incomplete without frolicking a bit with certain ethical notions. The opposite proposition could also be true.

I am not suggesting that a mutually exclusive connection exists between ethics and ontology. These two ideas are unique, although they often overlap. Important nuances still exist among them. The dissimilarities that exist among these ideas are still worth considering; we must do so as we go along in our discussions.

The existence of the being, as a unique entity, has little or no ethical implications as a single item. An examination of the being, on its own, does not automatically involve ethical concerns. Ethical notions come into play only when two or more beings interact in the same plane field. When my existence intertwines with someone else's, then my views of that *other being* or *beings* become relevant ethically and vice versa.

Such ethical considerations could take many forms. We could base them on individual values or they could emanate from the remnants [or the effects] of community values. But there ought to be at least two or more individuals interacting within the same setting before ethical concerns could become an important ontological issue.

Once ethics becomes a major point of interest, it might also become necessary to examine certain individual conducts[127] within the limits of those concerns. Ethics only plays a role in the being [or in the beings] when the individual enjoys the capacity to objectify others around him. Intersections among two or more individuals substantially involve ethical concerns.

COMMUNITY AND INDIVIDUAL VALUES

When Sartre speaks of human ontology, he makes out an obvious distinction between community

---

[127] Here, I am referring to human behavior.

Chapter 7. A Major Thinker

values and the individual opinions of what those values are or what they could be. In the look, Sartre argues that the being seeks to objectify everything or anything within his presence. Sartre inferred that the constant search for objectification is inherently ethical.

In Being and Nothingness, he writes:

"This woman whom I see coming toward me, this man who is passing by in the street, this beggar whom I hear calling before my window, all are for me *objects*—of that there is no doubt."[128]

The liaison between two individuals, most of all, incites a series of objectifications. Sartre contends, "The Other's presence to me is *object-ness*."[129] On the outset of this viewpoint, Sartre suggests that the being is seeking to objectify everything around him.

An existentialist examination proposes that the individual enjoys the freedom to subject others to his subjective scrutiny. That is, freedom allows the being the capacity to objectify others within his environment. The being has a duty to give essence

---

[128] Sartre, *Being and Nothingness*, 340.
[129] Sartre, 340.

to himself. In doing so, he must also deprive others of this essence.

That presence, as alluded in previous paragraphs, is precisely the foundation of Sartre's ethical concerns. "If this relation of object-ness is the fundamental relation between the Other and myself, then the Other's existence remains purely conjectural."[130] Sartre notes in the previously noted work, "My apprehension of the Other as an object refers me to a fundamental apprehension of the Other in which he will not be revealed to me as an object as a 'presence in person.'"[131] That idea, I argue here, would also invite ethical concerns.

Examinations that address moral principles could also help sketch the nature of Sartrean philosophy about ethics. Even though Sartre did not address these ethical concerns on their own, they appear crucial to his philosophical approach.[132] By it, they are also essential to my analysis. I must include them in this discussion.

---

[130] Sartre, 340.

[131] Sartre, 340.

[132] This is clearly in exergue in the book titled *"Being and Nothingness."*

Chapter 7. A Major Thinker

Ethics and ontology go hand and hand in Sartre's approach to the human project. But ethical notions seem more nuanced within the existentialist model.[133] To make such a claim, without reservations, is to fall within the same speculative mindset that pervades the literature, which I am trying to undermine here.

Prima facie, I do not have a straightforward answer about the reason Sartre saw the need for separating his works between ontology and ethics. Perhaps convenience was the only reason Sartre sought to elaborate on these principles on separate literary projects.[134] Granted, I may never find a

---

[133] My argument here centers on the notion that understanding the being requires an understanding of ethical ramifications. Ethics is not a stand along examination of the individual. The being must exist and must be aware of his existence in relation to others before ethics can become relevant. The being is first and ethics is only secondary. Existence precedes ethics. The continuity of existence indubitably implicates ethical concerns.

[134] It seems like Sartre was primarily concerned with deciphering the being before meddling into the ethical ramifications of its existence. Every facet of Sartrean ethics is interlaced with facets of human ontology. It makes sense to explore that ethics from an ontological standpoint. We could examine these two ideas on the same plane. They have much more similarities than disparities.

definitive proof to justify that viewpoint. It is likely that critics would regard my views as misguided.

It is still necessary to examine whether it is possible to examine a person's means of actions without affording an introspective look to his views about morality. Is there a way to study the rationale an individual might espouse in society or elsewhere without meddling into his moral values? From a Sartrean lens, the answer could only be no.

I propose a more positive scrutiny of the role ethical notions might have played in developing existentialism. I must admit it; this goal could only be achieved by evaluating Sartre's writings in *Being and Nothingness*. It is also relevant to examine how Sartre describes the essence of the individual in morality. I reckon that this is an ambitious undertaken. Still, it is a goal worth aiming for.

Examining all the works Sartre produced would be unlikely. Rather, the aim here is to survey some carefully targeted works about ethics. Assessing the Sartrean ethical imprint in the literature without appreciating the manner in which Sartre viewed the individual within his own environment could make our task impossible.

Chapter 7. A Major Thinker

It is important to examine the role of freedom in making up ethical choices. Ergo, it might be difficult to speak of a human ontology without appraising the practicable ways the being might construe his place in the environment. It could be impossible to speak of freedom without morality.

Ethical notions play a role in solidifying Sartrean philosophy. This understanding suggests that the Sartrean ethical ideals complement his views about existentialism. The existentialist model provides a much-needed rationale for deciphering Sartre's ethical concerns. We could regard ethics as an important facet of existentialism itself.

Furthermore, it is important to review Sartre's role in ethics based on the arguments echoed by opponents. It is supreme to highlight most of the claims that many often echo in the literature, which contest Sartre's role in ethics. There is a need to revisit some of the key arguments that are offered in Sartre's defense.

As you (the reader) move forward in this document, it should become obvious that I explored the claims that are often devised both in support and against Sartrean ethics. The goal is to cultivate a ground for a neutral approach.

Chapter Eight

Deciphering an Embedded Ethics

This chapter centers on the view that Sartre had a clear approach to ethics. It examines the view that Sartre was a prolific writer in the ethical domain. The chapter discusses the major arguments offered both in favor and against the idea that Sartre has an ethical dimension. It examines Sartre's viewpoints about ethics. It elaborates on the key arguments echoed in the literature.

8. A Prolific Writer

FACETS ABOUT SARTREAN philosophy have some undeniable ethical undertones to them. As previously noted, ethics is omnipresent throughout Sartre's philosophical ideals. Sartrean philosophy, on its own, does not need a separate examination or a thorough explanation of morality. Thus, we could examine the depth of Sartrean ethics through the lens of phenomenology.

Over his literary career, Sartre was a prolific writer. This is also true for his involvement in ethics, I would contend. His lavish role to this field

Chapter 8. A Prolific Writer

is irrefutable. Sartre's literary contribution to moral philosophy, however conservative it might be for critics, shows his commitment to developing a strong foundation for his ethics. For instance, Thomas Anderson notes that, throughout his career, Sartre developed various approaches to ethics.[135]

This scholar documented how Sartrean ethics developed in distinct phases.[136] Anderson notes that during his career, Sartre developed three distinct ethics. Figure 8.1 sketches the chronology of Sartre's approach to ethics.

These ethical mutations include an *idealistic* ethics (*Being and Nothingness*, 1943), *materialistic* and *realistic* ethics (*Critique of Dialectical Reason*, 1960), and *power* and *freedom* (tape-recorded interviews given to Benny Levy).[137] I discuss this facet of Sartrean ethics in another publication. Please refer to the book titled *Sartrean Ethics* to learn more about my position on these issues.

---

[135] Anderson, *Sartre's Two Ethics*.

[136] Anderson, 2.

[137] Anderson, 2–3.

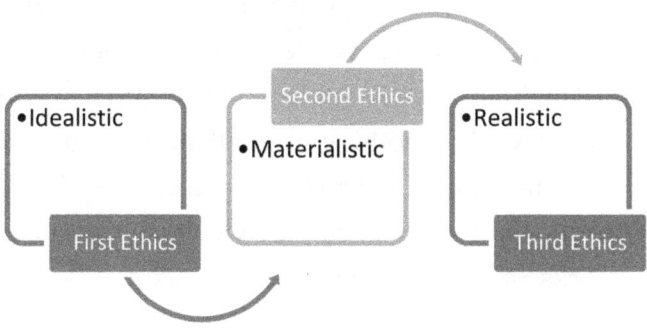

Figure 8. 1: Sartre's Three Ethics

The previous statements show that Sartre built up an ethical framework or (at least) he was close to completing it. The intimation that denies a Sartrean role in ethics is in error. Thus, the belief that insinuates that Sartrean ethics lacks a theoretical foundation is mistaken or perhaps it is misguided.

Refuting Sartrean ethics could be an unwise approach to finding out the role Sartre played in this literary discipline. Granted, Sartrean ethics is fragmented and incomplete. While I do not refute this viewpoint per se, I am uncertain that it frames a sound basis to rebuke Sartre's works in the field.

Those who embrace this view to undermine Sartrean ethics are mistaken. Saying that the

Chapter 8. A Prolific Writer

arguments Jean-Paul Sartre proposed in his writings about ethics are irrelevant. Such a view highlights a limited understanding of these works. Such a view is nothing else but suppositions about the materials Sartre produced. We could understand such a view as views about the many works Sartre published over the years.

SARTRE AND HIS INTIMATE PRECEPTS

It has been over three decades since Sartre passed away. Few people would deny that his intimate canons about the being are still relevant. His approach to human ontology radically changed the world. Sartre approached ethical issues from a humanistic portico. The understanding is that, "Ethics, for him, was fundamentally humanistic."[138] Sartre singlehandedly influenced the world and created a new model to examine its inhabitants.

We could make the argument that modern society is entrenched with the ideals Sartre proposed. Regardless of criticisms, existentialism is

---

[138] Anderson, 1.

still the cornerstone of contemporary understandings about the nature (or the extent) of human freedom in the world. Sartre sought to "construct a morality that was true to the human reality."[139] In that spirit, Sartre succeeded in this demarche.

Whether you share the preceding beliefs, Sartre clarified his most intimate surveys about the essence of the being. Sartre assessed the role of freedom in ethics in a consistent or concise manner. Sartre discernibly showed that human freedom is intertwined with the values the individual chooses.

Such venerations frame the foundation of society itself.[140] Setting up human values sets up the nucleus of modern understandings about human conducts. That is the reason it is relevant to examine how Sartre sought to resolve the impetuosity of ethics within the human project itself.

---

[139] Anderson, 1.

[140] Sartrean approach to freedom is the undergarment of various social ideas, including notions pertaining to individuality and the laws that protect and/or govern human conducts in society.

Chapter 8. A Prolific Writer

Sartre incited the ideas that reduced the influence of religion or God in many peoples' lives. Sartre argues that human beings have no nature; they are free to decide their own existence. Thus, it could be said that *"existence precedes essence."*[141]

There is no God in the Sartrean world. But we could say that ethical concerns played an important role in the way Sartre examined the being within his environment. We could regard ethics as a substitute for God in the Sartrean world.

SARTRE'S ROLE IN ETHICS

The intellectual theme in Sartrean philosophy is that men are responsible for who they are and what they will be in the world.[142] Nonetheless, there is an important distinction between individual freedom and individual conducts. One is the forerunner of the other, Sartre argues. But which one is it? Sartre was uncertain about which one induced the other.

---

[141] "Existential," accessed July 26, 2015, http://philosophy.lander.edu/intro/sartre.html.
[142] Ibid.

On the ethical plane, freedom guides human conducts, Sartre hints. Ontologically speaking, the need for freedom is the source that guides human conducts. The individual responds to his wish to be free. All the same, such a want or need for freedom begets undeniable ethical concerns.

Actions that spawn individual conducts might also bring about the need for freedom. There is a symbiotic connection between the two ideas (human freedom and human conducts). As the individual « *Surgit* » or *"Bursts"* into the world, he may proclaim his freedom from the world itself. Thus, the actions that the being does [or the actions the being must undertake] to uphold his freedom precipitate ethical concerns.

Let us say that immediately after a person was born, he/she has little or no understanding of the need for freedom. Physiologically, mentally, and psychologically, the being is incapable of such a role. However, as the individual evolves within the environment, he becomes aware of the constraint that granted his beingness.

Whether those constraints are from nature [or from society] is another question, which might compel further inquiries. Sartre proposes that the

Chapter 8. A Prolific Writer

being begins to nourish a need to break free from the grips of his environment. What is missing [or what is uncertain] is whether the need for freedom is induced by the environment or whether another mechanism brings about such a need?

It is always apt to examine Sartre's approach to ethics based on his examination of the individual. But we must do so specifically on the ontological plane. Likewise, it is important to explore how Sartre examined individual conducts. It is important to understand how he sought to link human conducts to human freedom. It is also necessary to understand how freedom affects human conduct. This examination would lead to a better appreciation of Sartre's moral philosophy in substance.

LOGISTICAL IMPEDIMENTS

Examining the extent of Sartrean ethics, from the proposed angle here, might pose some logistical impediments. One could not review every single works Sartre ever produced in the search for his ethics. It would be easier to appreciate that ethics in a more suitable medium. This is perhaps the reason Sartre sought to dedicate a separate literary project to elaborate (perhaps specifically) on his ethical concerns.

We could not ignore all the works Sartre produced about ethics. Even so, the corpus of his philosophical repertoire is great. There are places in these works where his ethical concerns are more obvious. But critics, before anything else, refuse to afford Sartre any positive treatment in the field. Sartre's potential role in ethics is almost wiped out by criticisms.

The views resounded in the literature suggest that Sartre has little or no intellectual merit in ethics. As noted earlier, there is ample evidence to suggest the contrary. One could evoke several arguments to support the view that Sartre played an important role in laying down an ethical outline in his major works. That outlook is chiefly based on the popularity of his philosophical brand. In that sense, it is important to examine the obvious association between phenomenology and ethics.

Refuting Sartrean ethics could be tantamount to refuting Sartrean philosophy altogether. Sartre's contribution to contemporary philosophy and, by extension, ethics, is distinct; it should not be undermined.[143] In making the previous claims, I reckon that most critics are not of a similar opinion. Still, there is a need to underline the reason we must afford an appreciative look to Sartre's role in this literary discipline.

Sartre was a sedulous thinker. His role in ethics deserves a more positive scrutiny. It is not fair to minimize Sartre's analytical approaches on the premise that he could not set up his ideas satisfactorily. There is more to Sartrean ethics than a mere inspection of the observations Sartre incited in his writings. I will examine this facet of the debate in following pages.

SUMMARIZING MAJOR CRITICISMS

Both Sartrean scholars and other commentators often note that Sartre failed to incorporate a true human ethics in his philosophy. While Sartre publicized his objects to delve in the ethical discipline, commentators are quick to point out he

---

[143] James Giles, *French Existentialism: Consciousness, Ethics, and Relations with Others* (Rodopi, 1999).

did not live up to this promise. The argument is that the works published posthumously on Sartre's behalf are inadequate to afford Sartre any recognition in ethics.

I do not dispute the preceding logic per se. Even so, we could revisit the major tenor of Sartrean ethics in other places, more specifically by exploring his literary works on the subject. I opted for a better scrutiny of Sartrean ethics by adopting a similar approach.

Let us focus on the works logged by a handful of intellectuals in the domain. Let us incorporate the works of several Sartrean scholars. These scholars are well vested in the topic; they are respected in their fields. Their scholarship and their analytical authenticity are beyond question.

The fundamental issues I hope to echo here center on the extent of the works Sartre produced about ethics. There is a need to refute the notion that Sartre did not contribute to ethics. But critics point out that, although Sartre promised to dedicate his next literary project to ethics, he never realized his ideas, at least not to his satisfaction.

Many commentators argue that Sartre was a failure in ethics. Some critics note that Sartre

Chapter 8. A Prolific Writer

perhaps worked tirelessly to realize that feat. But he abandoned, post hoc, his goals to write a book about moral philosophy, critics said.[144] This view, I gather, falls within the speculations I seek to denounce in the present work.

No one knows the reason Sartre did not complete his works about ethics. In saying that, we assume that his views on the subject are incomplete or are independent of Sartre's own doing. Arguably, all hints suggest that Sartre was aware of the drawbacks of his works. But Sartre wanted to publicize his works on ethics in their current form. This shows that Sartre was confident of his writings. I am sure that he would have incontrovertibly defended his positions against ill-conceived criticisms.

Since Sartre passed away, thus, cannot defend his ideas, it is much easier to rebuke his relevance in moral philosophy haphazardly. Sartre can no longer defend his position. Therefore, it is more convenient for critics to mischaracterize the ethics that Sartre meant in his works, considering his

---

[144] Gail Evelyn Linsenbard, *An Investigation of Jean-Paul Sartre's Posthumously Published Notebooks for an Ethics* (Edwin Mellen Press, 2000).

absence to defend his viewpoints. This is wrong, I am certain.

I do not share the belief that Sartre was a failure in ethical literature. I do not agree that his ethics lacked substance directly because his works appear unpolished or uncompleted. Opponents afford too much emphasis on the publication argument. We could examine Sartrean ethics antithetically.

The next few chapters make the case even more pronounced in favor of Sartre. They examine the scope of Sartre's major philosophical ideas. They tie existentialism with ethics. They disentangle Sartre's major claims. The goal is to highlight that Sartrean ethics is in integral part of Sartrean philosophy.

It is important to relay the effects of dissenting approaches against the viewpoints Sartre echoed in his works. To note a previous viewpoint, Sartrean ethics is not perfect. It is not my intention to suggest otherwise here. Nevertheless, denying that such an ethics is worthy of note by refuting the existence of Sartrean ethics altogether is intransigent.

Chapter 8. A Prolific Writer

SECTION 3

ONTOLOGY AND ETHICS

This section explores the link between Sartrean ethics and Sartrean philosophy. It explores the tentacles of Jean-Paul Sartre in moral philosophy. It examines the essence of his grandeur as a major thinker. The section reviews facets of his major works, including the role of God, freedom, temporality, and bad faith. It explores the degree to which Sartre contributed to ethical writings. It examines the views logged by several scholars.

Chapter Nine

Sartrean Philosophy

This chapter explores Sartrean ethics. It examines the views expressed against the notion that Sartre's approach to ethics has little or no literary relevance. The chapter sets up a connection between Sartre's approach to morality and human ontology. It revisits the role of freedom in fermenting moral values. The chapter assesses popular ideas in Sartre's works, including, bad faith, temporality, being and non-being, and the role of God in inciting individual actions. The chapter discusses the following notions: contingency, spontaneity, and the extent of the ideas known as the "for-it-self" and the "in-it-self."

9. Philosopher of the Century

JEAN-PAUL SARTRE IS among the best-known philosophers of the last century.[145] His ideas had a serious impact on philosophical writings. His works and his outlook about the quintessence of human existence helped create a new intellectual contrivance to understanding human beings in their environment (that is, in nature or in society).

---

[145] Flynn, "Jean-Paul Sartre."

Chapter 9. Philosopher of the Century

Sartre's approach to human ontology is also a philosophy of liberty. He was fixed about the power of the consciousness. Sartre underlined his positions about the sovereignty of the consciousness.[146]

This approach to philosophy is based on the power, the capacity, or the conditions of the individual to act or to omit certain actions without compulsion. At all stages of his life, Sartre had been a fierce defender of freedom. But his version of freedom is routinely based on conceptualizing subjective responsibility.

Under a Sartrean path to human existence, the being has the supreme power to control his actions. The subject is in charge of the choices he makes. Many consider Sartre the father of the « *L'Existentialisme athée Français* » or the *"French atheist."*

Sartre's works about life and freedom, from his acclaimed book *"Being and Nothingness,"* irrefutably transcended popular understandings about *"being"* or *"non-being."* His writings, in the ontological sense, inspired many philosophers for a good

---

[146] Ranwez, *Jean-Paul Sartre's Les Temps Modernes, a Literary History, 1945-1952.*

portion of the twentieth century. Let us explore his major works. Let us also examine the extent of his literary tentacles and the Sartrean legacy further.

THE BASIS OF SARTREAN ETHICS

Sartre wrote extensively about his ethical concerns. But only a few scholars nourish a similar understanding.[147] Only a few commentators regard Jean-Paul Sartre as a consequential moral philosopher.[148] Why that is the case? I am not sure how to answer this question.

For most critics, Sartre has little or no relevance in ethics. His works in philosophy, principally with his publications about existentialism, contradict his ethical concerns. I disagree.

The preceding presumption is the basis for most criticisms against Jean-Paul Sartre. This view also makes up the pillar of argumentations refuting

---

[147] Thomas C. Anderson, *Sartre's Two Ethics: From Authenticity to Integral Humanity* (Chicago, Ill: Open Court Publishing Company, 1993).

[148] Ronald Aronson and Adrian Van Den Hoven, eds., *Sartre Alive* (Detroit: Wayne State University Press, 1991).

Chapter 9. Philosopher of the Century

the Sartrean approach to moral philosophy. But Sartrean ethics is dynamic. Sartre had several approached to morality.

The gist of Sartre's moral thoughts evolved overtime. The Sartrean signature trademark to ethics transcended periodically through several phases. This transformation occurred during Sartre's long and fruitful literary career. The pervading understanding in most circles is that the main ideas of Sartre's moral philosophy are slanted into two major ethics or in two phases. As noted in the preceding chapter, there is an early ethics; there is also a contemporary ethics.

The impressiveness of Sartrean ethics is based on two major works: (1) his *"Notebooks for an Ethics;"* (2) hundreds of unpublished manuscripts of public lectures, which Sartre gave in 1964. These lectures include works that Sartre prepared to deliver in following years.[149]

Thomas Anderson notes that a Sartrean early approach to ethics is intrinsically idealistic.[150] But observers view little or no distinctions between

---

[149] Anderson, *Sartre's Two Ethics*.

[150] Joseph S. Catalano, Good Faith and Other Essays: Perspectives on a Sartrean Ethics (Rowman & Littlefield, 1996).

Sartre's early ethics and the views he espoused at a different point in his career. Still, such a link is not that obscure.

It is true that a Sartrean view on ethics, at least early in his career, was more radical and unapologetic. There is also a social or historical distinction to be made about Sartre's own thinking about morality overtime.[151] Sartre was entrenched in his ideas about human relations in their environment. On the other hand, as Sartre matured and evolved as an intellectual, his ethical *weltanschauungs*, some might say, and his understandings metamorphosed into different phases.

In the beginning of his literary works, Sartre was strict. Later in his career, he appeared more subdued and was willing to bend his own ideas a little bit to accept popular ways of think about the thoughts he once defended and championed. This approach to ethics is regarded as *realistic* (please refer to Figure 8.1).

The arguments often featured in the literature suggest that Sartre had no idea about how to insert

---

151 Ibid.

Chapter 9. Philosopher of the Century

ethics in the works he compiled about ontology. In the early days of existentialism, Sartre was spirited about his thoughts. Opponents contend that he did not exigently have a clear direction in mind. Nonetheless, it is not obvious whether Sartre was laying the foundation for a genuine ethics in his philosophy or whether his views grew parallel to a serendipitous creation of an ethics.

Thomas Anderson seemed unconvinced about the intellectual basis of Sartre's early moral thoughts. As admitted by most critics, Sartre produced a large amount of writings in the field.[152] Those works contained rich and detailed suggestions about an array of topics that are related to morality.[153] For Anderson, these works were not devised for ethics per se.

Anderson further notes that Sartre stressed in his prior works, human beings are free. They are unconstrained within nature itself.[154] Overtime, Sartre's early positions about freedom varied. Anderson also recognized that social causes might affect the Sartrean approach to human freedom in

---

152 Ji, "Freedom."
153 Ibid.
154 Anderson, Sartre's Two Ethics.

many facets. He admits that Sartre became more aware of the role of external forces onto human freedom.

Despite arguments to the contrary, Sartre changed and adapted his ideas in many ways. But he never abandoned his central thesis, other observers echoed.[155] There is a facet of clarity, cogency, or unity in Sartre's thoughts.[156]

Sartre remained committed to his ideas throughout his intellectual growth, even though he was willing to go soft on them. But Sartre never abandoned his views about the role of ethics in human conducts. Thus, the theorization that ethics and freedom work in tandem in Sartrean philosophy is not a farfetched understanding.

MORALITY AND FREEDOM

Is there a clear link between morality and freedom? Most pundits are not sure. At this point in our discussion, it is correct to state translucently that

---

[155] Ji, "Freedom."

[156] Catalano, Good Faith and Other Essays.

Chapter 9. Philosopher of the Century

the foundation of Sartrean philosophy centers on the notion of freedom. Let me elaborate further.

Sartre has always insisted on the conviction that the individual is always free until his death.[157] The individual is free, even if he were not to recognize that freedom. Could there be true freedom, when the being is bound by his moral values?

There is the likelihood that morality could be incompatible with notions of freedom. Ethical notions suggest that human beings are also bound by certain principles, which needs the individual to forgo his own judgment to that of a moral authority. To the points recorded by many observers, freedom would be in direct conflict with any notions of ethics or morality.

There is an argument to be made about the principles that guide human conducts in the world. These principles emanate from moral maxims. Moral values guide the nature of human ethics.

Ethics supersedes human conducts. By extension, ethics (that is, an ethical concern) kindles human freedom. The foundation of morality or

---

[157] Ji, "Freedom."

morals is based on limits, which, in turn, is based on supreme principles and standards that guide human conducts.

Likewise, human conducts are notarized by the customs, norms, values, and the virtues that a particular society, group, or faction has espoused overtime. The individual is the product of that environment and vice versa. The line between the effects of the environment onto the being or the manner in which the being responds to the environment is based on both individual ethics and community ethics. Please refer back to Chapter 7. There, I discussed the rapport between the individual and the community, as it refers to ethics, in greater length.

If we were to accept the previous assertion as true, it would mean that human beings are not free after all. That likelihood would also go against any notion that freedom guides human ethics. If human beings were independently free, as Sartre expressed, it might not be the case that their actions are predicated on any sense of morality or moral values.

In the same vein, if we were to argue that ethics precedes essence, we would have to admit that

Chapter 9. Philosopher of the Century

ethics also precedes existence. But there is also the possibility that ethics could precede both existence and essence. This debate is perhaps for another book project.

The Sartrean notion about morality does not erase the tragedy the individual must face, while construing his reality. Rather, it captures that reality. Otherwise, the being could not burst in the world without appraising himself and others within that world. To do that, he must base this assessment from a point of departure. That point, if it were to exist, could only be appreciated on the ethical plane.

The foundation of Sartrean philosophy lies on the role the individual plays in construing his freedom through moral values. From here, ethical notions and principles about human freedom play a significant role in Sartrean philosophy. A point of departure for freedom is ethics and vice versa.

It seems logical to argue that notions about freedom and morality go hand in hand. Until we could resolve whether a priori being or an entity is responsible for human existence, the best explanation is that a link exists between morality and freedom. To echo, there is more to freedom.

At first blush, Sartre did not explore the intricacies of this idea. As I mirrored in previous chapters, this examination is outside the scope of the present volume. Let us explore, though in short here, how Sartre examines freedom with ethics.

BEING AND NON-BEING

A Sartrean approach to human ontology suggests that the entity that is known as the *"individual"* is divided into two parts: the *"being"* and the *"non-being."* In the immediate structure of the *"for itself,"* Sartre sought to set apart the reason people are fleeing or the reason they engage in *bad faith*.

Sartre argues that the individual can be reluctant to admit his failure in life.[158] The being resorts to bad faith to cope with the reality within his environment. That reluctance, I would contend, is egocentrically ethical.

Phenomenology is about the link between the object and the subject. This rule could also be

---

[158] Thomas W. Busch, "The Philosophy of Jean-Paul Sartre" (Class Lecture, Villanova University, Spring 2014).

Chapter 9. Philosopher of the Century

appreciated as a direct experience.[159] The *non-being* is the opposite or a contradiction of the being. In this case, the being is undifferentiated.[160]

In the being for itself, the being is subjective. From this angle, it is the being of subjectivity. The being lacks of identity. To put it in other terms, the being is a witness to itself.[161] The individual is both the decider and the executor of his wants and need. It must also be noted that whichever direction he chooses could have ethical ramifications.

By contrast, the being is a presence to itself. According to Sartre, there is a need to understand the link between *non-positional* and *self-consciousness*. The individual is implicitly self-aware. The being acts a certain way within the environment itself. What guides individual actions could intertwine with the way the being makes out himself within the environment itself.

The question becomes, what could separate the being from itself. Sartre argues that there is a distance or a cleft that keeps the being apart from

---

[159] Ibid.
[160] Ibid.
[161] Ibid.

self-awareness. He refers to this crack as the *"non-being."*

For Sartre, there is nothing at the heart of the *"for itself."*[162] The individual splits within the self. The being is always in charge of that self. As a summation, the being is in charge of the self within the environment. This understanding also presumes that ethics is always an important idea to consider when examining the being in the milieu, be it social or natural, where the being evolves.

---

[162] Ibid.

Chapter 9. Philosopher of the Century

CHAPTER TEN

DESTINY, FREEDOM, AND GOD

This chapter delves in depth in various facets of Sartrean philosophy. It examines the role of God in simplifying or in hampering human freedom. The chapter explores the notion of temporality and the degree to which bad faith prevents the individual from being free. The chapter also examines viable paths to human freedom, including morality.

10. The Role of God

JEAN-PAUL SARTRE NOTES THAT individual actions are contingent. Spontaneity is an important facet of being in the environment. Under other conditions, there is no predictability or destiny.

For Sartre, there is no God. No one other than the being could fix his actions. Sartre argues that the presence of a God would undermine spontaneity.

God is the only interference in the freedom that the being could experience. God would prevent the being from acting contingently or fortuitously. As

Chapter 10: The Role of God

an alternative, God would be a total elimination of contingency.

Sartre argues that God is not good for freedom. The likelihood for a supreme being like God would undermine every facet of individual freedom. God creates the possibility for structure, order, and direction. God creates certainty. The individual would no longer respond to his wants or need. Thus, the being would no longer be able to burst into the world. Rather, the individual would be preprogrammed to act a certain way.

From that understanding, the being would not be responsible for his actions, which would in turn cut out the need for ethics. God is not compatible with human ethics. God is incompatible with freedom, Sartre notes.

Freedom and morality are intertwined. When the being is free or when he has the capacity to be free, he is the sole instigator of his actions in the environment. Individual freedom also involves ethical concerns.

As it happens, God is bad for freedom. God is diametrically contradictory to being free.[163]

---

[163] Ibid.

Certainty cuts out spontaneity. If there were a God, then there would be no freedom.[164] Likewise, if there were no freedom, there would be no essence. There would be no morality or ethics.

In trying to explain how phenomenology is important, Sartre argues that the *"for-it-self"* and the *"in-it-self"* could only be understood in the ontological plane. Sartre's goal is to prove that there is no determinism.[165] Phenomenology "seeks the essence of its subject matter: the essence of consciousness, the essence of perception, the essence of a physical object and so on."[166]

The being is trying to be God. But he may never succeed in this effort. Ethics or morality is the only line that keeps the individual in check.

Any adhesion to certain moral values may prevent the being from acting a certain way in his environment; it might induce certain behaviors, which we could construe as right or wrong. Ethics has the effects of both inducing and preventing the

---

[164] Sartre, Being and Nothingness, 788.

[165] Ranwez, *Jean-Paul Sartre's Les Temps Modernes, a Literary History, 1945-1952*.

[166] Stephen Priest, *The Subject in Question: Sartre's Critique of Husserl in The Transcendence of the Ego* (Routledge, 2002), 2.

individual (or the being) to act or from acting a certain way within the environment itself.

Temporality

Based on the idea known as temporality, it could be said that the being is struggling to settle his identity in the world. Sartre argues that time is the breakup of identity (or a reflection). There are two kinds of reflection: *pure* and *impure*. Reflection is a recuperative effect to gather the self into stasis.

The individual has to capture himself in action to give reason to himself. Whenever the being tries to capture him (self), he loses himself. This is a constant back and forth, which allows the individual the capacity to capture and nourish his freedom.

Pure reflection is an undistorted way to recognize oneself.[167] We could grasp this reality as a simple presence, recognition, revelation, or discovery. On the other hand, we could understand impure reflection as a distorted reflection.[168]

---

[167] Busch, "Sartre."
[168] Sartre, Being and Nothingness, 223.

The worst thing that could happen to an individual is when he is being subjected to external scrutiny by others. The individual may also become subject to his own examination. He (the individual) is said to be subjective. That subjectivity, as it happens, has some inherent ethical ramifications.

Temporality is a dispersion of identity.[169] Fusion breaks up that identity. The reflection can be deciphered as a constant effort by the individual to recover the consciousness. The being is also trying to get to the heart of the spontaneity, which would allow him to burst out of the moment. The possibility for a break or a cleft between the being and the non-being can turn spontaneity into a lack.[170]

Sartre further argues that life itself is a failure. Such a failure is that life, not necessary the biological understanding of living in the world, is unattainable. For Sartre, the infeasibility of life is unsustainable within any social environment. Sartre conceptualizes useless and unhappy

---

[169] Busch, "Sartre."
[170] Ibid.

Chapter 10: The Role of God

conscious. He does this to depict the state of individual life.

Emotion, by contrast, is a strategy the individual or the being develops to deal with the unattainable characteristics of life.[171] When the individual refuses to admit such unfeasibility, he finds himself in bad faith. Sartre argues that bad faith prevents the individual from being free.

BAD FAITH [MAUVAISE FOI]

Bad faith is a magical way to react to the failure of life. Here, bad faith is introspectively ethical. The individual convinces himself that he can be himself in the mode of identity.[172]

The individual chooses a persona. He thinks that he can become that persona in his mind. The individual can deceive himself. As well, he can believe in the identity he created for himself.

To be in the in-itself, the individual must not be aware that he is deceiving himself and that he has created a new identity for himself in the world.

---

[171] Ibid.
[172] Ibid.

Then, the being must be oblivious that he has taken a new persona. The individual must be unconscious of his efforts to deceive himself. Ethics, in this case, community values, is the only buffer that could prevent the individual from acting in ways that could hinder freedom, with reservations for other individuals within the environment.

In bad faith, people create an alternative world for themselves. They believe in the world that they created. Realizing that life is unattainable, they act in a way so they could complete their selves.[173] That reality involves ethical concerns. Thus, bad faith suggests morality, a firm sense of values—whether it is individual values, collective values—, or the lack of that.

PATHS TO FREEDOM

Sartre argues that there are two paths to freedom: a *"break-up"* or *"non-being"* and *"being."* We can break with bad faith, as long as we desire to do it. The

---

[173] Ibid.

Chapter 10: The Role of God

individual could try to stay away from his past. From a phenomenological lens, for instance, the individual could say, I am – I am not my past.[174]

The individual could try to ignore his past or he could try to create a cleft from the past. For the being, the past hunts the present. There must be continuity. Sartre calls the past the *"in-itself"* or *"stasis."*[175]

Sartre does not want us to think of ourselves in ways we could make out as determinant (or cause and effect). Freedom allows the individual the capacity to break away from the past and be free in the present. For Sartre, this is an eternal back and forth.[176] But what does that mean?

We escape from identity to return toward identity in the immediate future. That is what Sartre refers to as a flight from the past toward the future.[177] The individual is falling from one identity toward another identity. As he navigates that difficult phase of being, ethics becomes the only compass that can guide him through the world.

---

[174] Sartre, Being and Nothingness, 172.

[175] Busch, "Sartre."

[176] Ibid.

[177] Ibid.

Chapter Eleven

The Sartrean Legacy

This chapter reviews the legacy of Jean-Paul Sartre. It points out the works Sartre compiled about ethics. The argument here is that, even though some of the works Sartre produced are obscure or uncompleted, they should not be ignored for these reasons. This chapter centers on the arguments offered against existentialism as a major theory, including inciting ethics as an impediment for human freedom. This chapter reiterates the view that there is a symbiotic link between morality and freedom.

11. A Universal Thinker

JEAN-PAUL SARTRE WAS a universal thinker. His intellectual impacts are without precedents. Sartre's views about individual freedom or human existence are not empty of dissenting opinions.

Critics devalue the Sartrean literary contribution to philosophy and ethics for no tangible reasons. Some opponents sought to classify Sartre as a confused thinker. This view is grounded on the supposition that Sartrean philosophy, in all its glory, is disjointed and contradictory.

Chapter 11: A Universal Thinker

With ethics, opponents argue that Sartre did not provide us with an ethical work. He did not provide an outline of his claims, which would make it possible for us to grasp his views about ethics. Some say that there is no way to find out what that ethics looks like or what such an approach to ethics would sound like.[178] From this angle, the view often repeated by most observers, pundits, and commentators alike, is that Sartre does not have a clear ethical foundation in his works. This argument includes the works that Sartre produced or published while alive and other works, which had been released posthumously.

To say it again, these criticisms are misguided. They are based on a distorted assessment of Sartre's works in ethics. Sartre compiled several writings on ethics, even though they are incomplete. Please refer to the publication titled *"Sartrean Ethics: A Defense of Jean-Paul Sartre as a Moral Philosopher"* to learn more.[179]

Let me highlight, though summarily here, the views espoused by several observers, namely

---

[178] Ji, "Freedom."

[179] Johnson, *Sartrean Ethics*.

prominent Sartrean scholars, who agree that Sartre provided valuable insights about his ethics throughout his career. I will try to prove that Sartrean ethics is not as elusive as critics prevailingly claim.

EXISTENTIALISM UNDER ATTACK

Divergent understandings about Sartrean ethics often extend beyond Sartre's capacity to develop an ethical outline in his works. Critics attacked Sartre's intellectual ingenuity to develop a genuine philosophy. Many opponents levied that Sartrean philosophy is pessimistic and indulges the individual to a road of despair and inaction.

Others also contended that Sartrean philosophy would lead the individual to overlook the value of the solidarity of humankind. But Sartre argues that human ontology is based in self-deceptions.[180] Because this depiction of the human reality is unflattering, he has been charged with misrepresenting the human experience.[181]

---

[180] Becker and Becker, *Encyclopedia of Ethics*.
[181] Ibid.

Chapter 11: A Universal Thinker

Sartre was aware of those who espoused a dissenting approach to his philosophy. He derisively responded to his critics by inferring that they were incapable of grasping his writings. Granted, there is an argument to be made here.

Sartre did not radically aim at depreciating the human experience; rather, he sought to venerate it. He sought to flatter us.[182]

Sartre's response to his most avid detractors typically centers on the viewpoint they did not read his works carefully. Sartre refused to be blamed for inaccurate readings of his works. But Sartre admitted that his philosophy could lead to negative connotations or could have negative impacts on those who do not fully grasp his ideas.

Sartre's response to his opponents often comes across as being contemptuous. As proof, he routinely cautioned his most ardent readers [or his critics] not to engage in superficial readings of his texts. Such an *"on-the-surface"* approach to his writings, Sartre echoed, might not reveal the

---

[182] Ibid.

positive and optimistic message he is trying to suggest in them.[183]

THE LINK BETWEEN ETHICS AND FREEDOM

Critics refuted any link between human ontology and morality. Most observers regard Sartrean ethics as an impediment to master freedom itself. Sartre offered a narrow perspective to ethics in general, some say. Critics argue that the Sartrean ethical reflections led to a negative approach to ethics. The underpinnings of a Sartrean ethics denigrate the responsibility of the individual in setting up his own freedom.

A Sartrean slant to ethics denies the possibility for freedom, critics argue.[184] The centerpiece of Sartrean ethics is the prolegomenon of human

---

[183] Nigel Warburton, "A Student's Guide to Jean-Paul Sartre's Existentialism and Humanism | Issue 15 | Philosophy Now," accessed July 17, 2015, https://philosophynow.org/issues/15/A_students_guide_to_Jean-Paul_Sartres_Existentialism_and_Humanism.

[184] Patrick Engel, "Negativistic Ethics in Sartre," *Sartre Studies International* 19, no. 1 (June 1, 2013): 16, doi:10.3167/ssi.2013.190102.

Chapter 11: A Universal Thinker

freedom; this is also the unifying thread of the existentialist's major contribution to ethics.[185] For many observers, this understanding is, without any elaboration, inadequate. Critics retorted that the Sartrean *Modus Operandi* (or M.O.) Examining human freedom could not effectually explain the ramifications of morals or moral maxims in society.

In Sartre's way of exploring human conduct and his viewpoints of ethical issues underline the power of men to construe morality at their discretion.[186] Sartre refuses to accept the role of nature in creating a standard of human conduct or a universal framework for understanding moral virtue, which most men aspire to reach. Sartre rejects the contemplation that a priori moral rule, which can be understood as human nature [or God himself], guides human behaviors in every facet of their lives.

Sartre was anti-God. He does not believe in the presence of a higher power, which controls human dealings within the natural environment.[187] For

---

[185] Ji, "Freedom."
[186] Ibid.
[187] Ibid.

most commentators, this is precisely where a Sartrean ethics crumbles on its own weight.

Many believe that a Sartrean agency toward human freedom does not care to explain where the individual earned his capacity to be free. In effect, this is an important point of contention. For the sake of brevity, however, I did not address this facet of the debate here. Again, this discussion is perhaps for another writing project.

Morality and Existentialism

Assuming that the consideration that freedom is only a facet of Sartrean philosophy, would there be a link between morality and existentialism. In the section about morality and freedom, I contended that a clear link exists between ethics and freedom.

At this point, it is worth reiterating that critics universally see such a likely link as poles apart. From their vantage point, there is no link to be had between the two ideas. If there would be any connection, it would not favor the idea that freedom guides ethics or vice versa.

Chapter 11: A Universal Thinker

Sartre does not reject the role of morality in freedom or in human existence altogether. He believes that moral aphorisms are framed individually and are spilled over towards the community. Yet, for most critics, the extent of an overarching morality remains dubious when it comes to individual freedom.

There could be no morality, if there ought to exist the possibility for freedom. Within that context, Sartre argues that morality is the domain of men. Throughout his writings, Sartre proves that men themselves create their own version of morality and values.[188]

The Sartrean view about human ethics suggests that the individual plays an important role in setting up his own ideals about morality onto the rest of the world. There is a need to examine the ramifications of bad faith, as it applies to ethics, within the notion of morality. It seems supreme to discuss the importance of bad faith within the context of human freedom and human conduct.

From a Sartrean lens, bad faith is the bridge between men and their capacity to enjoy freedom

---

[188] Ibid.

in nature. Bad faith comes from the person's intransigence to accept his reality. We could best analyze that intransigence through ethics.

The major principles of a Sartrean approach to ethics assume that an individual's intransigence is the root of alienating his freedom. The individual is the instigator of his destiny; he also foments his freedom. Thus, he must realize this freedom.

Sartre proposes his existentialism doctrine as the best means to help the individual overcome this intransigence, which often leads to bad faith. At the heart of his writings, Sartre suggests that ethical concerns are omnipresent in the way individuals sets up their role in the environment where they develop or function. In this case, ethics is a primitive element in individual conducts.

To put it in another term, we can make out Sartrean ethics in the manner in which the individual senses his capacity to construe his role within the environment. There is no point in arguing whether Sartrean philosophy does not have a clear outlook about the onset of ethics in human existence. That ethics is not that elusive.

It should be obvious that ethics and human ontology go hand-and-hand. To echo a previous assertion, there could be one without the other. Notions about ethics and existentialism complement each other.

IMPORTANT POINTS OF DISPUTE

David Pellauer made several arguments against the extent of Sartrean ethics. In the publication titled *Sartrean Ethics*, I discuss the different arguments that are often intimated to refute Sartrean ethics.[189] In this instance, however, it is worthy of note that Pellauer unambiguously refutes, what he makes out as the aberration, that Sartre had a downright developed theoretical approach to his ethical concerns in his works.

Let us revisit several diatribes Pellauer levied against that ethics. These claims are based on the following understandings:

◙ Such a project was inherently impossible.

◙ No ethics can be had in Sartrean writings, when considering that the foundation of that ethics

---

[189] Johnson, *Sartrean Ethics*.

lies on describing intersubjectivity, as developed in the book *"Being and Nothingness."*

◉ The general outlines of a Sartrean ethics are not always perceptible.

◉ A Sartrean ethics is impossible, if one were to move beyond the limits of *Being and Nothingness*.

◉ While Sartre does offer several interesting discussions about several topics relevant to ethics—namely an ethics developed based on his ontology—what we know about this ethics is not enough to make up a real point of departure for a genuine ethical idea.[190]

Pellauer argues that current discussions about the Sartrean approach to ethics, which he translated in the book « *Cahiers pour une morale* » or *"Notebooks for an Ethics,"* are only useful as a stimulus to further thoughts. Any overall synthesis is lacking in the present ethical montage of Jean-Paul Sartre, he notes. Again, I disagree.

Pellauer seems convinced that a Sartrean approach to ethics is elusive. He intimated that an analysis of a Sartrean ethics is matter-of-factly

---

[190] Sartre, Notebooks for an Ethics.

Chapter 11: A Universal Thinker

unattainable.[191] For Pellauer, Sartre does not deserve the title of a moral philosopher. As noted previously, this view is erroneous. It is important to prove the flaws in Pellauer's approach.

Philosophy and Sartrean ethics intertwine. My view of Pellauer's appreciation of Sartrean ethics is plain. Pellauer is straight out on the wrong end of Sartre's legacy in moral philosophy. His depiction of that ethics is inaccurate.

Pellauer misread or he misinterpreted some arguments Sartre echoed in his notebooks. I refute Pellauer's viewpoints. I provided enough evidence here to cement my most relevant claims on the matter.

To reiterate, Pellauer is in error. I am convinced that his assessments about Sartre's works about ethics are misguided. In my view, Pellauer is lost in the translation about the extent of Sartrean ethics.

The arguments I incited here might seem trivial to critics. But to explore the issues in depth, let us rely on the views explained by Sartrean experts. There is a need for productive criticisms towards Sartre.

---

[191] Ibid.

Chapter Twelve

Productive Criticisms

This chapter centers on the positive arguments often devised by critics in favor of Sartrean ethics. It elaborates on the need for a better approach to that ethics. The chapter talks about the role the individual plays in fermenting his own moral virtue in the environment. The chapter discusses the extent to which a genuine human ethics is sketched in Sartre's major works. It elaborates on the views that offer a neutral approach to the Sartrean ethical model.

12. Sartre and his Fewer Supporters

SEVERAL TYPES OF CRITICISMS are often evoked against Jean-Paul Sartre. As already noted, many of the disparagements levied against Sartre are in error. I outlined a few observers who logged positive pointers to support the existence of Sartrean ethics. In the following pages, I will elaborate on the reason(s) I argue that the Sartrean approach to ethics deserves a better scrutiny.

It is not right to overlook or undermine the Sartrean contribution to ethics, considering that

Chapter 12: Sartre and his Fewer Supporters

criticisms are based on misguided views. Criticisms often seek to devalue Sartre's true intellectual valor. This is not right, I would contend.

In response to such misguided criticisms, it is important to explore the postulations that are often offered in favor of Sartrean ethics. Sartrean ethics is not that inconsequential in the literature. There is a need to take Sartre's writings in this domain seriously. Let me elaborate on this viewpoint.

Let me note that not everyone ferments a disparaging view about Sartrean ethics or Sartrean philosophy. For example, Mann Anika argues that there are reasons within society that affect the ontological conditions of human beings.[192] Sartre believes that the early motivation an individual might have towards realizing a genuine ethics depends on the environment in which he evolves or the reality the individual finds himself. To explain this view in different terms, what will post hoc bring about ethical concerns depends on the link the being experiences in the environment.

A Sartrean outlook to ethics is based on the view that Sartre neglected the role of objectivist

---

[192] Anika Mann, "Sartre's Ethics of the Oppressed," *Philosophy Today* 49 (January 1, 2005): 105.

elements in human freedom.[193] Thus, the Sartrean ethical model does not consider the role of external causes. From this lens, opponents consistently argue that Sartre is not concerned with the role of social causes on human conducts.

There is the understanding that a genuine human ethics habitually lies solely within subjected people.[194] Because conquered people are the ones to whom oppression is originally disclosed, it is up to them to find their pathway toward a genuine human ethics.[195] This view is on par with the intimation that the individual always enjoy freedom, regardless of the circumstance he finds himself.

Human understandings about the role of morality are construed at an intrinsic level. There is a tacit state of acceptance or a bond of complicity between the oppressed and the oppressor, which affects the ontological conditions of the oppressed.

---

[193] David J. Detmer, "Freedom as a Value: A Critique of the Ethical Theory of Jean-Paul Sartre (Existentialism)" (Northwestern University, 1986).

[194] Mann, "Sartre's Ethics of the Oppressed."

[195] Ibid.

Chapter 12: Sartre and his Fewer Supporters

Unless extraordinary circumstances arise, this reality hinders a human ethics.[196]

In the oppressed-oppressor rapport, the individual construes his role to one another. Oppressors cannot provoke an ethical society so long as the oppressed have not aimed for it. The oppressed must take action that would lead toward an ethical society.[197] These criticisms are without question misdirected.

Contrary to the preceding viewpoints, Sartre considers the role of external causes. He recognizes that the eventual instigator of an ethics is the individual. The individual is responsible (and holds the capacity) for understanding the environment in which he develops. We must consider several ethical ramifications. Such implications are worthy of acknowledgement here.

The decision to act or to omit to act does not depend on the external forces, which may act on the individual. Freedom affords the individual the capacity to construe his reality and to settle the correct course of action. The individual is free to

---

[196] Ibid.
[197] Ibid.

interact with the external causes that govern his existence in any way he considers it acceptable or necessary. Thus, the individual is always free to accept or to reject his reality or life circumstances.

LINKING EXISTENTIALISM WITH ETHICS

Despite the recriminations assessing the manner in which Sartre examined ethical problems, opponents also challenged Sartre's views on various facets, including his signature theory, existentialism. The question posed here is whether it is possible to talk about Sartrean ethics without examining existentialism. The answer is no.

Most critics refuse to link existentialism with ethical notions. Several scholars questioned the need for an ethics is only about the ontology of the being. They question the possibility that there could be an ethics, when the individual enjoys an incommensurable amount of discretion or latitude. From that understanding, there can be no human ontology when the individual has the ultimate power or the capacity to act or to prevent the self from bringing about certain actions.

Chapter 12: Sartre and his Fewer Supporters

The theoretical underpinning of existentialism is rambling, they say. It does not account for overarching moral realities or societal conditions. Any other way, the existentialist model does not jibe with ethical notions. Critics propose this argument as a pretext to undermine Sartre's role in moral philosophy. This viewpoint about criticisms against Sartre is not in the majority though.

Other observers express an unconventional approach to the issue. From their angle, a marriage between existentialism and ethics would make perfect sense. Such an amalgam, they argue, would work, insofar if we were to rely only on notions about the existentialist model to examine the core of Sartrean ethics.

The compatibility between the two ideas is obvious, critics assume. Freedom, as an individual value, underlies both the subjectivist and the objectivist undertone of Sartrean ethical thoughts.[198] Freedom is tied with subjectivism.[199] Thus, there is no doubt that an individual ethics is an important part of the existentialist model.

---

[198] Detmer, "Freedom as a Value"; Detmer, "Review."

[199] Detmer, "Freedom as a Value."

It is worthy of note that certain charges about Sartrean ethics are mixed. I labored to examine the different arguments that are often offered both in favor and against the extent of Sartrean ethics. I tried to remodel, although summarily, some views projected in the literature. I did so as succinctly as possible.

The issues might still be complicated for some of you. But let us explore the nature of that ethics a bit further to make sense of it. Let us examine mixed views about the influence of Sartrean ethics.

MIXED REVIEWS

In the book titled *Sartrean Ethics*, I explored several of the arguments voiced by a few observers in Sartre's favor.[200] They include Thomas Anderson, Robert Stone, and Elizabeth Bowman. Here as well, I referenced the views echoed by these authors, markedly in previous sections.

Many of these scholars do not refute the likelihood that Sartrean ethics is incomplete. They

---

[200] Johnson, *Sartrean Ethics*.

Chapter 12: Sartre and his Fewer Supporters

also recognize that such an approach to ethics has some intellectual merit. Their assessment of that ethical model is mostly positive.

All the same, I do not refute their position either in the present text. I will clarify facets of their arguments. I will explore the claims they logged in Sartre's favor.

There is no objectivity here. I take sides in the debate. But I do so based on the views pointed out by the scholars. I highlight some indictments that these critics offered both in support and against Sartre. Still, I do so as neutrally as possible.

Based on the discussions noted in this manuscript many people disagree that Sartre has a rightful place in ethical literature. Others went even further; they sought to disprove Sartrean philosophy altogether. A third group is worthy of note here.

These scholars espoused a more neutral position about the extent of Sartrean ethics. They did not reject a Sartrean role in ethical writings; they did not seek to rebuke the usefulness of Sartrean philosophy either. Instead, these observers recognized the synergy of ethics in the Sartrean philosophical mechanism. They also pointed out obvious flaws in the way Sartre set apart ethical issues.

My analysis in the book titled Sartrean ethics examined the works of these scholars. My position in the present text is also based on the views expressed by these thinkers.[201] Their approach is more convincing for several reasons. Here, let us examine two reasons.

First, they applauded Sartre's efforts to distillate a concise approach to human ethics. Second, they tried to resolve inconsistencies in the ideas Sartre noted throughout his works. They also sought to clarify disparate positions and irreconcilable ambiguities in the writings Sartre produced. The text (Sartrean Ethics) was rigorously tailored to capture the views scattered by these scholars.

Anderson, Stone, and Bowman are among the best-known authors and *distinguished* scholars in Sartrean philosophy. They examined Sartre's works extensively, outstandingly about ethics. They published several literary materials about the appropriateness of Sartrean ethics. Their take on the issue is relevant, as I sought to show here.

---

[201] Johnson.

Chapter 12: Sartre and his Fewer Supporters

It needs to be reiterated that this publication is not a disowning of Jean-Paul Sartre's moral philosophy. It is not an acclamation of his larger approach to human ontology. In contrast, this book is not intended to offer added supports to popular critics. I have reservations about the notion that existence takes precedence over essence. But this disputation is for another literary project.

This work was not designed to highlight blindly only the arguments offered in Sartre's favor. Rather, the ideas advanced here are designed to help solidify the inference that Sartre is a moral philosopher in many ways. Sartre played a substantive role in ethical writings.

The central theme voiced throughout this exposé is that Sartre has a rightful place in ethics. He is an incommensurable contributor in this discipline. Depriving him of the title of a moral philosopher is not fair.

Sartre's writings about ethics are more extensive than previously credited. It is more marked than the views critics expressed in the literature. Hence, criticisms that seek to undermine Sartre's intellectual merit are misplaced.

There are other ways to quantify, judge, and exhaustively settle the weight of Sartrean ethics. Despite the many drawbacks that plague the Sartrean approach to moral philosophy, Sartre highlighted an irrefutable *"examination"* of his ethical concerns. Denying this fact is unpretentiously wrong, if not unethical, I would denote here.

A Philosophical Bequest

Ethics is the gateway to understand Sartrean philosophy in its most epistemological foundation. A Sartrean perspective to ethics may offer a glimpse into the intellectual construction of Jean-Paul Sartre's literary wealth. Thus, grasping the chief constituent of Sartrean ethics is important to appreciate the breadth of his contribution to the literature.

A Sartrean philosophical legacy is incommensurable. Jean-Paul Sartre's unfettered literary contributions to humanity are incontestable. The Sartrean approach to ethical

Chapter 12: Sartre and his Fewer Supporters

issues is not always revered or accepted under positive terms.

I sought to explain that a link exists, though not expressly, between Sartrean philosophy and his approach to ethics. His published documents on the subject depict his ideals energetically. Recognizing one facet of Sartre's works while ignoring the ethical ramifications that are set in within those writings, some might say, does little to advance his literary legacy.

It is important to note that Sartrean ethics is not perfect. Nonetheless, it is also paramount to cast the flaws of Sartrean ethics in the fairest lights. Rebuking the Sartrean approach to ethics without recognizing the role or the implications of individual conducts within the existentialist model is inaccurate. This could only lead to misinterpreted notions about Sartre's true contributions to moral philosophy. This would eventually minimize the value of Sartrean philosophy or his role in human literature altogether.

Ben Wood Johnson

THE CASE FOR A DUAL APPROACH

The best way to study Sartrean ethics is through the lens of phenomenology, mainly through human ontology. To do so, I must admit, we must test the strength of the arguments that seek to refute Sartre's works. Few criticisms are based on the substance or the intellectual merit of Sartre's works. But refuting arguments often center on the quantity of the works Sartre produced (for example, the publication argument).

Critics also note that such works could serve as points of reference to examine the real ethical foundation of Sartre's writings. I do not refute that approach here. I must point out that existing arguments are conjointly one-sided; they are most likely based on the content of Sartre's works, rather than the argument intimated in such compilations. Still, I am convinced that no real criticisms could nullify the extent of Sartrean ethics.

Anyone can levy criticisms against a writer, heedfully if such criticisms are based on the contents of a particular work. Criticism is a subjective effort. A literary critique does not

Chapter 12: Sartre and his Fewer Supporters

permanently settle whether a work is worthy of any intellectual appreciation. A criticism would not characteristically subtract or add value to a particular piece of work. It is just an opinion, an individual examination, or a collective understanding of a craft.

Even when a critic, a pundit, or a commentator does not hold the epistemological credence to criticize a particular work or a topic, he might still have a valid argument about the content of the work he is analyzing. In this case, I afford more credence to criticisms that are based on the quality of a piece of literary work in philosophy.

I, overall, argue in favor of a substantive scrutiny of Sartre's works. My arguments center on the idea that few commentators examined Sartre's works substantively. Several facets of Sartrean philosophy are related to ethics. It is equally necessary to afford a greater credence about arguments that are offered to support the existence of a genuine Sartrean ethics.

There is an unbreakable link between Sartre's views about human existence and morality. Therefore, the foundation of existentialism is intertwined with ethics. Absorbing the reach of

Sartre's views about morality would also implicate a thorough evaluation of human ontology.

ACHIEVING MY GOALS

My objective in this text was to help you [the reader] cater a greater understanding about the link that invariably exists between existentialism and ethics. It is important to grasp the many issues that collectively underlie Sartrean ethics. It might be impossible to grapple with ethics or the Sartrean approach to the concept without recognizing or even incorporating important criticisms about existentialism.

Another goal here was to highlight the major themes of Sartre's past works in moral philosophy. I wanted to examine facets of the arguments that are often postulated both in support and against the Sartrean approach to ethics. I wanted to explain that criticisms are often in error.

I also sought to assess the extent to which the kinds of reprobation or rebuttal voiced in the literature could help settle whether Sartre played a genuine role in moral philosophy. Criticisms are

Chapter 12: Sartre and his Fewer Supporters

not thorough enough to rebuke Sartre in ethics. Such criticisms are too subjective. In this case, we could appraise their intellectual essence as dubious.

You might still have questions about the role Jean-Paul Sartre played in moral philosophy. You might even be more confused than before. But there is more to Sartrean ethics than most people realize. This text only scratched the surface of the issues.

You might be unhappy with the arguments I outlined here. Again, let me reiterate that this text is an addendum to a previous book about Jean-Paul Sartre. Please refer to my other publications to learn more about my arguments.

The next segment outlines the key viewpoints I echoed throughout the present document. It reinforces my position about the role Sartre played in ethics. This portion revisits the most relevant views indexed in the literature. It outlines the views echoed to deny Sartrean ethics.

There are many dissenting views against Sartre. The most obvious claims often target Sartre directly or personally. Critics are likely to examine the major principles of *Existentialism*. We could regard such criticisms as inconsequential to undermine

Sartre. The intellectual merit of Sartrean ethics is irrefutable.

Ill-conceived criticisms, taken together, seek to refute the arguments, which Sartre proposed in his works about ethics. Critics refuse to recognize any link between human ontology and morality. I disagree with such criticisms. There is a need for a positive appreciation of the works Sartre produced in ethics.

I may never know whether I convinced you that Sartre deserves a role in moral philosophy. Whether I persuaded you that my arguments have any weight in the debate, is up to your disposition to accept that Sartre played a role in the ethical discipline. But I hope I was able to change your perspective about Jean-Paul Sartre. If not, I hope I was able to solidify your positive viewpoints about Sartre, however slightly that it might be.

Sartre deserves more recognition as a moral philosopher. His legacy in the ethical genre is under attack. There is a need to defend this great thinker. I hope you share a similar view.

Chapter 12: Sartre and his Fewer Supporters

FINAL WORDS

CLOSING THOUGHTS

This portion of the manuscript outlines my concluding thoughts. It includes several data about the works Jean-Paul Sartre produced during his career, notably some of the most relevant terms he habitually echoed in his works. This part contains an index and a brief bio (about the author).

The e-Book does not include any appendix and an index.

Conclusion

THROUGHOUT THIS EDITION, I strove to present a favorable facet of Jean-Paul Sartre. I sought to stress his role on ethics. Whether I succeeded in this demarche is another question.

I would rather leave the preceding question unanswered. Perhaps you, as the reader, are best suited to judge. I will leave it up to you to evaluate the effects of my claims or even the intellectual relevance of my efforts.

What is plain are the arguments featured in this text. I explored several claims in this work. But none of them, I echoed, offers irrefutable evidence to support the premise that Sartre does not deserve the title of a moral philosopher. My examination of the literature yields to one conclusion. That is, Sartre is an accomplished moral philosopher.

Despite the many viewpoints to the contrary, the existence of Sartrean ethics is unmistakable. His role in the field is irrefutable. Thus, Sartrean ethics is alive and well.

Regardless of the views often noted in the literature o rebuke Sartrean ethics, that ethics is worthy of an intellectual recognition. Sartre set up his ethical concerns in a pronounced format. There is no need to read between the lines.

Granted, Sartrean ethics is not perfect. I can understand the reason observers classify such works as disjointed and incomplete. I do not argue otherwise. Not even Sartre would dissent.

SARTRE IS STILL ALIVE

Jean-Paul Sartre is still a major player in modern literature. There is no way critics could refute that the Sartrean contribution to modern philosophy is unparalleled. Sartre's works are resourcefully vital. They are relevant for today's literary consumption.

The preceding understanding is a point that several scholars made during the 1990s, mainly via the book titled *"Sartre Alive."*[202] I would say that, even in 2016, Sartre is still a relevant thinker in moral philosophy. Sartre is still alive; he is still relevant in literature.

Opponents are fixed about Sartre's role in ethics. They are quick to refute that Sartre had an influence in this domain. David Pellauer notes that Sartre announced at the end of *"Being and Nothingness"* that he would devote his following works to ethics. Contrary to Sartre's own expectations, Pellauer argues, this was an unfulfilled promise.[203]

The previous argument is a powerful indictment, which is often precipitated by most

---

[202] The book Sartre Alive was published in 1991. It was a collaborative effort of various scholars in the field. There were approximately 17 authors/contributors to the organization of the publication. The book covered several topics, including ethics, which was developed by Robert Stone and Elizabeth Bowman. There was also another section on ethics, which had been developed by Thomas Anderson.

[203] Jean-Paul Sartre, "Notebooks for an Ethics" (1992).

Conclusion

pundits as a means or a strategy to refute Sartrean ethics. But this view is wrong. Sartre devoted his following works to ethics. This reality is irrefutable.

Sartre published a book titled *Notebooks for an Ethics*, which, ironically, was translated from French into English by David Pellauer. Claiming that Sartre did not fulfill his promise is outrageous. This is inconceivable, if not ethically questionable.

The preceding view results from an inaccurate assumption about the extent of Sartrean ethics. This analysis claims to explain what Sartre intended in his unfinished works. This outlook is also echoed in almost every criticism contradicts with Sartre.

Critics are convinced that Sartre is not a moral philosopher. I disagree with that assessment. I am not the only person who regards Sartre's role in ethics from such an angle.

Several commentators are more sympathetic towards Jean-Paul Sartre. They adopted a more conscientious stance towards the intellectual worth of Sartre's works in ethics. While they regard as a failure the works that Sartre did not complete, they also suggest that we could understand this failure as a testament of Sartre's success.

Alain Ranwez notes that Sartre's philosophical enterprise is unquestionably and remarkably ambitious.[204] It is the most radical and inventive undertaken within the twentieth century.[205] Scholars like Ronald Aronson and Adrian van den Hoven went further. They coined the term *"Sartre's Exemplary Failures"* to point out the reason Sartre never completed his major projects.[206]

From these scholars' vantage point, we could understand Sartre's failure from a larger perspective. They argue that Sartre tried to interject himself in so many incompatible literary disciplines all at once that his failure to carry out his goals should not be seen as a failure in the true sense of the word. They note:

"Sartre attempts to remake every genre and every discipline to which he is attracted, whether it is the novel, theater, biography, psychology, or Marxism. In retrospect, we can see that a certain project *was* impossible. Sartre had the boundless

---

[204] Ranwez, *Jean-Paul Sartre's Les Temps Modernes, a Literary History, 1945-1952*.

[205] Ranwez.

[206] Ronald Aronson and Adrian Van Den Hoven, eds., *Sartre Alive* (Detroit: Wayne State University Press, 1991), 25.

Conclusion

energy and (nearly) blind courage to try; his failures, consequently, are as exemplary as his successes."[207]

These scholars note that Sartre did not complete almost all his major works, including his ethics, Flaubert, *Critique of Dialectical Reason*, and *Roads to Freedom* — almost all of his major projects of the 1940s, 1950s, and 1970s.[208] Still, they do not see Sartre himself as a failure. They assimilated Sartre's uncompleted works as "efforts to do the impossible; it was a way to reconcile the irreconcilable," they echoed.[209]

There is the argument that Sartre did not publish a book or any relevant materials in the field. This is an outlandish viewpoint. This depiction of Sartre's writings is hardly accurate. Sartre was active in ethics. There is ample evidence to support that assertion.

Along similar viewpoints, critics sought to classify Sartre as a failure in ethics. Sartre's involvement in ethics predates his rise to literary stardom with the book *"Being and Nothingness."*

---

[207] Aronson and Hoven, 26.
[208] Aronson and Hoven, 25.
[209] Aronson and Hoven, 25.

Even throughout the 1960s, he was active in ethics. Thus, criticisms against Sartrean ethics are misguided.

There is a little *"bad faith,"* I would argue, by most critics against Jean-Paul Sartre. Even when critics recognized that Sartre compiled materials relevant to ethics, they refute those works. I argue for a different approach toward this legacy of ill-conceived criticisms.

Sartre deserves the recognitions he is due, at least as a moral philosopher. His ethical concerns are clear in his major works. Sartre's most influential ideas about human ontology seem empty and incomplete when analyzed in a vacuum. They are shallow without considering important ethical concerns.

CENTRAL THESIS

The arguments I echoed here center on the notion that critics must recognize that ethics is omnipresent in Sartre's major literary oeuvres. Deciphering that ethics does not fall within a mystery, as pundits suggest. There is a need for a

Conclusion

better examination of Sartrean ethics. There is a need for a holistic approach. Perhaps this is the best way to appreciate that ethics.

I refute the view that Sartre is not a philosopher in ethics only because his approach is empty of a theoretical foundation. The theoretical foundation of Sartrean ethics stems from his approach to human ontology. But critics often overlook that fact.

In the Sartrean world, there could be no human ethics without grasping the extent of human ontology. It could be difficult to exclude existentialism from the Sartrean perspective to moral philosophy. Put another way, the link between Sartrean philosophy and Sartrean ethics is unbreakable.

One is a subset of the other. From a larger scheme of things, the link between phenomenology and ethics is inextricable. It is not always clear which comes first. Sartre struggled with these notions unsuccessfully.

The term ethics, in its most epistemological sense, suggests philosophy. We could understand ethics as a branch of philosophy. It could be difficult to detach this concept of ethics from phenomenological ontology.

A symbiotic bond exists between the two ideas (that is, ethics and ontology). Sartre understood that link. He professedly expressed such a link eloquently, if not fluently, throughout his many works, notably his compilation about ethics. He did so in both published and unpublished materials. Thus, denying Sartrean ethics, to echo, is unabashedly unethical.

Conclusion

BIBLIOGRAPHY

Anderson, Thomas C. "Sartre's Early Ethics and the Ontology of Being Ad Nothingness." In *Sartre Alive*, 183–201. Detroit: Wayne State University Press, 1991.

―――. *Sartre's Two Ethics: From Authenticity to Integral Humanity*. Chicago, Ill: Open Court Publishing Company, 1993.

Appignanesi, Lisa. "Did Simone de Beauvoir's Open 'marriage' Make Her Happy?" *The Guardian*, June 10, 2005, sec. World news. http://www.theguardian.com/world/2005/jun/10/gender.politicsphilosophyandsociety.

Conclusion

Aronson, Ronald, and Adrian Van Den Hoven, eds. *Sartre Alive*. Detroit: Wayne State University Press, 1991.

Bair, Deirdre. *Simone de Beauvoir: A Biography*. Simon and Schuster, 1991.

Benewick, Robert, and Philip Green. *The Routledge Dictionary of Twentieth-Century Political Thinkers*. Routledge, 2002.

Bernstein, Richard J. *Praxis and Action: Contemporary Philosophies of Human Activity*. University of Pennsylvania Press, 2011.

Boulé, Jean-Pierre. *Sartre, Self-Formation, and Masculinities*. Berghahn Books, 2005.

Busch, Thomas W. "The Philosophy of Jean-Paul Sartre." Class Lecture, Villanova University, Spring 2014.

Campbell, W. John, and Jean-Paul Sartre. *No Exit and The Flies Notes*. John Wiley & Sons, 1983.

Dobson, Andrew. *Jean-Paul Sartre and the Politics of Reason: A Theory of History*. Cambridge University Press, 1993.

Drake, David. "Sartre, Camus and the Algerian War." *Sartre Studies International* 5, no. 1 (1999): 16–32.

Flynn, Thomas R. *Sartre: A Philosophical Biography*. Cambridge: Cambridge University Press, 2014.

Fraser, Mariam. *Identity Without Selfhood: Simone de Beauvoir and Bisexuality*. Cambridge University Press, 1999.

Fullbrook, Kate, and Edward Fullbrook. *Simone de Beauvoir and Jean-Paul Sartre: The Remaking of a Twentieth-Century Legend*. Harvester Wheatsheaf, 1993.

Giles, James. *French Existentialism: Consciousness, Ethics, and Relations with Others*. Rodopi, 1999.

Johnson, Ben Wood. *Sartrean Ethics: A Defense of Jean-Paul Sartre As A Moral Philosopher*. Eduka Solutions, 2016.

Judaken, Jonathan. *Jean-Paul Sartre and the Jewish Question: Anti-Antisemitism and the Politics of the French Intellectual*. U of Nebraska Press, 2006.

Linsenbard, Gail Evelyn. *An Investigation of Jean-Paul Sartre's Posthumously Published Notebooks for an Ethics*. Edwin Mellen Press, 2000.

McBride, William Leon, and Calvin O. Schrag. *Phenomenology in a Pluralistic Context*. SUNY Press, 1983.

McEwen, Todd, and Lucy Ellmann. "Damp Squibs." *The Guardian*, January 14, 2006, sec. Books. http://www.theguardian.com/books/2006/jan/14/highereducation.biography.

Conclusion

Meszaros, Istvan. *The Work of Sartre*. New York: Monthly Review Press, 2012.
O'Neil, Patrick M. *Great World Writers: Twentieth Century*. Marshall Cavendish, 2004.
Pace, Edward Aloysius, and James Hugh Ryan. *The New Scholasticism*. American Catholic Philosophical Association, 1970.
Pramaggiore, Maria, and Donald E. Hall. *RePresenting Bisexualities: Subjects and Cultures of Fluid Desire*. NYU Press, 1996.
Priest, Stephen. *The Subject in Question: Sartre's Critique of Husserl in The Transcendence of the Ego*. Routledge, 2002.
Ranwez, Alain D. *Jean-Paul Sartre's Les Temps Modernes, a Literary History, 1945-1952*. Whitston Pub. Co., 1981.
Rowley, Hazel. *Tete-a-Tete: The Tumultuous Lives and Loves of Simone de Beauvoir and Jean-Paul Sartre*. New York: Harper Perennial, 2006.
Sartre, Jean Paul. *Cahiers pour une morale*. Paris: Gallimard, 1983.
Sartre, Jean-Paul. *Being and Nothingness*. Translated by Hazel E. Barnes. Reprint edition. New York: Washington Square Press, 1993.
— — —. Notebooks for an Ethics (1992).
Sartre, J.-P. *Les Mots*. 1St Edition edition. Librairie Gallimard, 1964.

Major Works and Famous Quotes

This portion of the text includes Sartre's major works and famous quotes. It examines the most famous phrases Sartre often echoed in his publications. While the section is not exhaustive, it includes the most common words that Sartre used during his career.

A Prolific Writer

JEAN-PAUL SARTRE produced an array of literary materials, many of which had been released during his lifetime. Between 1936 and 1974, Sartre produced 34 books or manuscripts. He published on average one book each year.

Sartre was more prolific at times. In 1947, for instance, he published four items. The closest prolific years worth pointing out here include 1946 and 1965, when he published three items each year.

Other periods were marked by a slower, steady production. He published two items during the

A Prolific Writer

following years: 1939, 1945, 1949, 1956, 1957, and 1964. The years noted earlier were also productive, though not as much as the periods. At least, Sartre published one item each year while alive. Let us review some of those works in the next segments.

APPENDICES

THIS PART FEATURES several quotes, which form Sartre's literary trademark. These quotes include phrases, words, or sentences, which Sartre engineered himself or they are part of popular slangs he regularly uttered. This section reiterates the major thesis voiced in the book. The remaining portion of the text includes a bibliography and an index part.

Appendices

APPENDIX A: SARTRE'S MAJOR WORKS

SARTRE'S WORKS (POSTHUMOUS WORKS PUBLICATIONS)

Title	Year	Title	Year
The Transcendence of the Ego	(1936)	Existentialism and Human Emotions	(1957)
Nausea	(1938)	The Problem of Method	(1957)
Sketch for a Theory of Emotions	(1939)	Critique of Dialectical Reason	(1960)
The Wall	(1939)	Sartre on Cuba	(1961)
The Imaginary	(1940)	The Words	(1963)
Being and Nothingness	(1943)	Literature & Existentialism	(1964)
The Age of Reason	(1945)	Colonialism and Neocolonialism	(1964)
The Reprieve	(1945)	The Philosophy of Existentialism	(1965)
Existentialism and Humanism	(1946)	The Philosophy of Jean-Paul Sartre	(1965)
Anti-Semite and Jew	(1946)	Essays in Existentialism	(1965)
Morts sans sepulture	(1946)	The Family Idiot	(1971)
No Exit and Three Other Plays	(1947)	Between Existentialism and Marxism	(1974)
Baudelaire	(1947)	Witness to My Life: The Letters of Jean-Paul Sartre to Simone	(1983)

Major Works and Famous Quotes

		de Beauvoir, 1926-1939	
La Nausée	(1947)	Notebooks for an Ethics	(1983)
Existentialism	(1947)	Quiets in a War	(1983)
What is Literature?	(1948)	The Freud scenario	(1984)
Troubled Sleep	(1949)	"What is Literature?" and Other Essays	(1988)
Zeit der Reife	(1949)	Truth and Existence	(1989)
Saint Genet	(1952)	Jean-Paul Sartre: Basic Writings	(2001)
Existential psychoanalysis	(1953)	Conversations with Jean-Paul Sartre	(2005)
Life/situations	(1956)	Muertos Sin Sepultura	(n.d.)
Nekrassov	(1956)	Der Aufschub	(n.d.)
Lucifer and the Lord, a play in eleven scenes			(n.d.)

APPENDIX B: PUBLICATIONS WHILE ALIVE

PUBLICATIONS WHILE ALIVE

Year	Number of Publications
1936	1 Publication
1938	1 Publication
1939	2 Publications
1940	1 Publication
1943	1 Publication
1945	2 Publications
1946	3 Publications
1947	4 Publications
1948	1 Publication
1949	2 Publications
1952	1 Publication
1953	1 Publication
1956	2 Publications
1957	2 Publications
1960	1 Publication
1961	1 Publication
1963	1 Publication
1964	2 Publications
1965	3 Publications
1971	1 Publication
1974	1 Publication

Because this is the subject of the present publication, it is worthy of note that Sartre was

Major Works and Famous Quotes

very prolific even after death. Since Sartre passed away in 1980, he published several items that surely kept him alive and relevant, at least from an intellectual standpoint. Sartre's posthumous repertoire includes eight publications.

Between 1983 and 2005, Sartre published several posthumous works. The most prolific year was 1983, with three publications. Sartre released his most famous works on ethics that year. The book is titled *Notebooks for an Ethics*.

APPENDIX C: POSTHUMOUS PUBLICATIONS

POSTHUMOUS PUBLICATIONS

Year	Number of Publications
1983	3 Publications
1984	1 Publication
1988	1 Publication
1989	1 Publication
2001	1 Publication
2005	1 Publication

APPENDIX D: CONCEPTS AND QUOTES

JEAN-PAUL SARTRE (TWENTY FAMOUS WORDS OR CONCEPTS)

French Version	English Translation
1. *Mauvaise Foi*	Bad faith
2. *Liberté*	Freedom
3. *Choix*	Choice
4. *Néant*	Nothingness/nothing
5. *Project*	Project
6. *Contingence*	Contingency

Major Works and Famous Quotes

7. *Situation*	Situation
8. *Conscience*	Conscience
9. *Essence*	Essence
10. *Existence*	Existence
11. *Moi*	Self
12. *Destin*	Destiny
13. *Perception du monde*	World view
14. *Vécu*	Lived/Experienced
15. *Être-révèle*	Being Revealed
16. *Morale*	Ethics
17. *Subjectivité*	Subjectivity
18. *Objectification*	Objectification
19. *Rupture*	Break/Fissure
20. *Spontanéité*	Spontaneity

APPENDIX E: FAMOUS QUOTES

JEAN-PAUL SARTRE (FIFTY FAMOUS QUOTES)

French Version	**English Translation**
1. « L'enfer, c'est les autres. »	"Hell is for the others/Hell is other people." — Jean-Paul Sartre
2. « Jamais nous n'avons été plus libres que sous l'Occupation Allemande. »	"We have never been as free as under German occupation." — Jean-Paul Sartre
3. « L'existence précède l'essence. »	"Existence precedes essence." — Jean-Paul Sartre
4. « L'homme est une passion inutile. »	"A man is useless passion." — Jean-Paul Sartre
5. « Ce qui importe n'est pas ce qu'on a fait de nous, mais ce que nous faisons nous-mêmes de ce qu'on a fait de nous. »	"What is important is not what we did to ourselves; rather, the important is what we are doing to what we have done to ourselves." — Jean-Paul Sartre
6. « J'ai besoin de la souffrance des autres pour exister »	"I need the suffering of others to exist." —Jean-Paul Sartre, No Exit
7. « Quand je suis tout seule, je suis éteint. »	"When I am all alone, I am extinguished." — Jean-Paul Sartre, No Exit
8. « J'ai trouvé le cœur humain	"I found the human heart

Major Works and Famous Quotes

vide et insipide partout sauf dans les livres. »

empty and insipid everywhere except in books." — Jean-Paul Sartre

9. *« Le pire d'avoir été menti c'est de savoir que vous ne méritiez pas la vérité »*

"The worst part about being lied to is knowing you weren't worth the truth." — Jean-Paul Sartre

10. *« Le néant se trouve lové au cœur de l'être - comme un ver. »*

"Nothingness lies coiled in the heart of being - like a worm." — Jean-Paul Sartre, *Being and Nothingness*

11. *« La vie n'a aucune signification, du moment que vous perdez l'illusion d'être éternelle. »*

"Life has no meaning, the moment you lose the illusion of being eternal." — Jean-Paul Sartre

12. *« L'existence précède l'essence. »*

"Existence is prior to essence." — Jean-Paul Sartre

13. *« C'est seulement dans nos décisions que nous sommes importants. »*

"It is only in our decisions that we are important." — Jean-Paul Sartre

14. *« Votre jugement vous juge et vous définit. »*

"Your judgment judges you and defines you." — Jean-Paul Sartre

15. *« La vie est une passion inutile. »*

"Life is a useless passion." — Jean-Paul Sartre, *Being and Nothingness*

16. *« Tout ce qui existe et naquît sans raison, se prolonge par faiblesse et meurt par hasard. »*

"Every existing thing is born without reason, prolongs itself out of weakness, and dies by chance." — Jean-Paul Sartre

17. « On pourrait seulement endommager soi-même à travers le mal qu'on fait d'autrui. »

"One could only damage oneself through the harm one did to others." — Jean-Paul Sartre

18. « Un individu se choisit et se fait lui-même. »

"An individual chooses and makes himself." — Jean-Paul Sartre

19. « La mort est la continuité de ma vie sans moi... »

"Death is a continuation of my life without me..." — Jean-Paul Sartre

20. « Une fois que la liberté s'allume au cœur de l'homme, les dieux sont impuissants contre lui ».

"Once freedom lights its beacon in man's heart, the gods are powerless against him." — Jean-Paul Sartre

21. « Tous les hommes sont des prophètes, sinon dieu n'existe pas. »

"All men are Prophets or else God does not exist." — Jean-Paul Sartre

22. « L'homme n'est pas la somme de ce qu'il a déjà, mais plutôt la somme de ce qu'il ne dispose pas encore, de ce qu'il pouvait avoir. »

"Man is not the sum of what he has already, rather the sum of what he does not yet have, of what he could have." — Jean-Paul Sartre

23. « Divagations d'un fou sont absurdes en ce qui concerne la situation dans laquelle il se trouve, mais pas en ce qui concerne sa folie. »

"A madman's ravings are absurd in relation to the situation in which he finds himself, not in relation to his madness." — Jean-Paul Sartre, Nausea

24. « Qu'entendons-nous par dire qu'existence l'précède

"What do we mean by saying that existence precedes

Major Works and Famous Quotes

l'essence? nous entendons que l'homme tout d'abord existe, se rencontre, poussées vers le haut dans le monde- et se définit lui-même par la suite. »	essence? We mean that man first of all exists, encounters himself, surges up in the world-and defines himself afterward." — Jean-Paul Sartre, Existentialism Is a Humanism
25. *« Il n'y a pas la nature humaine, puisqu'il n'y a pas de divinité à concevoir. »*	"There is no human nature, since there is no god to conceive it." — Jean-Paul Sartre, Existentialism and Human Emotions
26. *« Un homme se sent rarement comme rire seul. »*	"A man rarely feels like laughing alone." — Jean-Paul Sartre, Nausea
27. *« J'existe, c'est tout. »*	"I exist, that's all." — Jean-Paul Sartre, Nausea
28. *« J'ai commencé ma vie comme je la finirai sans doute : au milieu des livres. »*	"I started my life as I will probably finish the: in the middle of books." — Jean-Paul Sartre, Les Mots/The Words
29. *« On meurt toujours trop tôt — ou trop tard. et cependant la vie est là, terminée : le trait est tiré, il faut faire la somme. tu n'es rien d'autre que ta vie. »*	"We always die too early — or too late." And however, life is completed: the stroke is drawn, it should be the sum. "You are nothing more than your life." — Jean-Paul Sartre, No Exit

30. « Alors c'est ça l'enfer. Je ne l'aurais jamais cru... vous vous rappelez : le souffre, le bûcher, le gril. Ah quelle plaisanterie. Pas besoin de gril, l'enfer c'est les autres. »

"So is it hell. I would have never thought it... You remember: suffers, the stake, grill... Ah, what joke? No need to grill, hell is other people." — Jean-Paul Sartre, Huis Clos/Les Mouches

31. « Faire souffrir c'est posséder et créer tout autant que détruire. »

"Hurt is similar to possessing and creating, as well as destroying." — Jean-Paul Sartre, Baudelaire

32. « Je prenais tout au sérieux, comme si j'avais été immortel. »

"I took everything seriously, as if I had been immortal." — Jean-Paul Sartre, The Wall

33. « J'étais un enfant, ce monstre qu'ils fabriquent avec leurs regrets. »

"I was a child, this monster they produce with their regret." — Jean-Paul Sartre, The Words

34. « Peut-on juger une vie sur un seul acte ? »

"Can we judge a life on a single act?" — Jean-Paul Sartre, No Exit

35. « Mais vous ressemblait beaucoup plus à un camarade qui avait juste rendu compte qu'il vit sur des idées qui ne paient pas. »

"You looked much more like a fellow who had just realized that he has been living on ideas that don't pay." — Jean-Paul Sartre, The Age of Reason

36. « Je ne suis ni le maître ni l'esclave, Jupiter. je suis ma liberté ! à peine m'as-tu créé que

"I am neither master nor slave, Jupiter. I am my freedom! Hardly you created

Major Works and Famous Quotes

j'ai cessé de t'appartenir. »

37. « *Jamais nous étions plus libres que sous l'occupation allemande.* »

38. « *J'admire la façon dont nous pouvons mentir, en mettant la raison de notre côté.* »

39. « *Seuls les actes décident de ce qu'on a voulu.* »

40. « *Mes souvenirs sont comme des pièces de monnaie dans le sac à main du diable : lorsque vous l'ouvrez vous trouverez des feuilles mortes seulement.* »

41. « *Croire est de savoir vous croyez, et pour savoir que vous croyez n'est ne pas de croire.* »

42. « *Célébrité, pour moi, la haine égale.* »

43. « *Un droit est rien de plus que l'autre aspect de l'obligation.* »

44. « *Je ne suis rien que le regard*

me I stopped you belong." — Jean-Paul Sartre, The Flies

"Never were we freer than under the German Occupation."
— Jean-Paul Sartre, The Aftermath of War

"I admire the way we can lie, putting reason on our side."
— Jean-Paul Sartre, Nausea

"Only acts decide what we wanted." — Jean-Paul Sartre, No Exit

"My memories are like coins in the devil's purse: when you open it you find only dead leaves." — Jean-Paul Sartre, Nausea

"To believe is to know you believe, and to know you believe is not to believe." — Jean-Paul Sartre

"Celebrity, for me, equals hatred"
— Jean-Paul Sartre, Existentialism Is a Humanism

"A right is nothing more than the other aspect of duty." — Jean-Paul Sartre

"I'm nothing that the gaze

qui te voit, que cette pensée incolore qui te pense. »

45. *« Quelque chose commence pour mettre un terme : l'aventure ne se laisse être étendue elle atteint signification que par le biais de sa mort. »*

46. *« Tu n'es rien d'autre que ta vie. »*

47. *« Le néant hante étant. »*

48. *« Lorsque vous êtes seul, vous êtes en mauvaise compagnie. »*

49. *« Je n'ai aucun besoin de bonnes âmes : un complice est ce que je voulais. »*

50. *« Je suis, je suis, j'existe, je pense donc que je suis ; je suis parce que je pense, pourquoi je pense ? Je ne veux pas penser plus. »*

Source: Goodreads.com

that sees you, that this colorless thought that you think." — Jean-Paul Sartre, No Exit

"Something begins in order to end: an adventure doesn't let itself be extended it achieves significance only through its death." — Jean-Paul Sartre

"You are nothing more than your life." — Jean-Paul Sartre

"Nothingness haunts being." — Jean-Paul Sartre

"When you're alone, you're in bad company" — Jean-Paul Sartre

"I have no need for good souls: an accomplice is what I wanted." — Jean-Paul Sartre

"I am, I am, I exist, I think therefore I am; I am because I think, why do I think? I don't want to think anymore." — Jean-Paul Sartre, Nausea

Please note that the above list is based on several items retrieved from the website known as www.goodreads.com. The quotes featured here were originally written in French. I retrieved them respectively from the aforementioned websites.

The current version is a literal English translation of these quotes. Also, be aware of mistakes or translation errors.

INDEX

BELOW IS A LIST OF some words that are repeated throughout this document. Please be advised that this index is not exhaustive by any means. It contains some of the most essential words that had been used in the book.

This index does not include a separate "subject" and "name" entries. Both items are listed conjointly throughout the index. Please refer to the table of contents for more information about a particular subject.

Index

The index is listed in alphabetical order. It also includes references pertaining to names, places, topics, and other information about Jean-Paul Sartre. It also contains information about other pertinent scholars. The index contains several key references and other useful terms.

Academic, 20–21, 30, 65
Academic crucible, 30
Academicians, 71
Academic interest, 20
Acclaimed, 1, 7, 91, 142
   Acclaimed book, 91, 142
   Acclaimed works, 7
   Acclaimed writer, 1
Accomplishments, 7, 10, 30, 32, 39
Achievements (see:
   Accomplishments)
Acknowledgement, 184, 200
Acolyte (see: Beauvoir, Simone de)
Acquaintance, 17, 109
Activism, 51
Activist (see: Politics - Political)
Admirers, 32–34, 72
Adulthood (see: Sartre)
Affaire (see: Romantic)
Agency, 173
Algeria, 52–53
Algerian conflict (see: Algerian war)
Algerian girl, 36
Algerian people, 12, 36, 52–53
Algerian war, 12, 52–53
   Algerian (see: Algerian people)
Aloysius pace, 33
Altona, 52
Ambitious, 119, 205

Anderson, Thomas, 109–10, 124, 126–27, 143–44, 146, 187, 189, 203
Anika, Mann, 182
Anne-Marie, 15–16, 18–19, 36, 91
   Majordomo, 19
Anti-Antisemitism, 31
Anti-God, 172
Antithetically, 135
Aphorisms, 174
Apolitical, 50
Appignanesi, Lisa, 24
Arlette-Elkaim, Sartre, 30–31, 36
Aron, Raymond, 58
Aronson, Ronald, 143, 205–6
Athée, 142
Athée français, 142
Atheist, 142
Authentic, 85
Authentication, 1
Authentic ethic, 85
Authenticity, 67, 83, 87, 109, 133, 143
Author, 30, 91–92, 187, 189, 203
Authority, 59, 92, 148
Autobiography, 17, 19–20
Baby (see: Jean-Paul-Charles-Aymard-Léon-Eugène)
Barionà, 48
Barnes, Hazel E., 30, 46

Beauvoir, Simone de, 21–25, 58, 91–92
Berlin (see: Germany)
Bernstein, Richard J., 62
Biography, 9, 15, 19, 23, 30, 91, 205
Bisexual (see: Beauvoir, Simone de)
Born-again writer, 19, 36
Boulé, Jean-Pierre, 35
Bowman, Elizabeth, 187, 189, 203
Broussais Hospital, 31
Busch, Thomas W., 5, 61, 151, 160–61, 164
Cahiers pour une morale, 112, 177
Campbell, John, 50, 54
Camus, Albert, 12
Career, 1, 10, 21, 25, 29–30, 54, 56, 58, 83, 112, 123–24, 144–45, 169
Catalano, Joseph S., 144, 147
Catros, Philippe, 45
Censorship (see: Germany - German - German occupation)
Chaplin, Charlie, 59
Character, 35, 92
Character assassinations, 92
Child, 15, 20, 30, 74
Childhood (see: Jean-Paul-Charles-Aymard-Léon-Eugène)
Circles, 14, 23, 31, 34, 72, 89–90, 144
Circumstance, 183–85
Civility and conviviality, 2
Civility, 2
Civilization, 14, 34
Colonialism, 12
Communism, 51
Condorcet (see: Lycée)
Contemporaneous, 14, 33, 144, 203
Contemporaneous philosophy, 33, 203
Cool (see: Hype)
Cornell university, 53
Cox, Gary, 48
Crabs (see: Drug)
Crépin, Annie, 45
Crowd (see: Funeral)
Cuba, 12
Darwall, Stephen, 75
Daughter (see: Elkaïm)
Death, 16, 18–19, 36, 148

Debauchery, 91
Despondent, 18
Destiny, 63, 155, 157, 175
Determinism, 159
Detmer, David J., 183, 186
Dewey, John, 74, 80
Dialectical, 124, 206
Dialectical reason, 124, 206
Diatribes (see: Pellauer, David)
Dilemma of sartrean ethics, 110
Dobson, Andrew, 50–51
Domestic, 52
Dominion (see: Germany - German)
Dramatist (see: Jean-Paul-Charles-Aymard-Léon-Eugène)
Drug, 48
Duplicity, 92
École, 21
Economics, 76
Écrits, 34, 36
Education, 10, 21, 25, 52
Educational institutions, 88
Ego, 159
Egocentrically, 151
Egotistical, 33
Elkaïm, 30–31, 36, 111–12
Ellmann, Lucy, 91
Embryonic, 5, 73
Enigma, 101
Epistemological, 191, 194, 208
Escort girl (see: Anne-Marie)
Ethics, 2–6, 11–14, 37, 51, 56, 61, 65, 67, 69–83, 85–90, 92–97, 99–102, 108–15, 117–28, 130–35, 137, 140, 143–51, 153, 158–59, 163–64, 166–69, 171–78, 180–97, 201–4, 206–9
Ethikos, 78
Ethos, 78
Etymology, 70, 74, 78
Europe, 44
Existence, 38, 62, 78, 105–7, 114, 117–18, 128, 135, 141–42, 149–50, 167, 174–75, 181, 185, 190, 194
Existential, 30, 32, 38, 42, 46, 50, 58, 61, 64–65, 75, 92, 99, 105–6, 113–14, 116, 118–20, 126, 128, 132,

Index

135, 143, 146, 166, 169, 171–73, 175–76, 183, 185–87, 192, 194–96, 208
Expertise, 73, 94
Experts, 178
Expert, 100
Famous, 30, 56, 74
Fans, 31
Fate, 64
Father, 15–18, 22, 30, 142
Fierce, 44, 142
Flaubert, 206
Flynn, Thomas, 15, 20, 30, 34, 45, 141
For-itself, 62, 99
For-it-self, 140, 159
Français, 25, 142
France, 15, 31, 43–45, 47, 50–53, 58–61, 64
  L'Hexagone, 46
Free, 12, 24, 63, 95–96, 98, 105, 128–30, 146, 148–49, 156, 158, 162, 164, 173, 185
Freedom, 19, 42, 47, 50, 62–64, 75, 88, 95–96, 98–101, 104, 116, 120, 124, 127–30, 137, 140, 142, 146–51, 155–60, 163–64, 166–68, 171–75, 183–84, 186, 206
French, 12, 15–16, 21, 31, 33, 39, 43–46, 48, 52, 59, 82, 91, 132, 142, 204
  French existentialism, 132
  French intellectual, 31
  French legion d'honneur, 39
  French literature, 12, 33, 48, 59, 82
  French military, 46
  French navy, 15
  French resistance, 43
Friends, 20, 22, 58
  Friendship, 21–22
Fullbrook, Edward, 22–23, 25
Fullbrook, Kate, 22–23, 25
Fulton, Ann, 46
Funeral, 31
  Fifty-thousand, 31
Fusion of the in-itself, 99
Genuine, 86, 88–89, 93, 97, 146, 169, 177, 180, 182–83, 194–95, 205
  Genuine ethics, 182

Gerassi, John, 48
Germany, 25, 43–44, 52
  German, 42–43, 45–48, 50, 52
  German forces, 46
  German invaders, 47
  German invasion, 46
  German military, 47
  German occupation, 42–43, 46, 49, 52
  German occupiers, 50
  German prison camp, 48
Girl (see: Anne-Marie)
Grandparents, 17
Greek word, 78
Green, Philip, 53
Hallucinogenic, 48
Hegel, Georg Wilhelm Friedrich, 80
Heidegger, Martin, 25, 49
Hexagon, 59
Hobbes, Thomas, 80
Holistic, 208
Household, 35
Housekeeper, 19
Hoven, Adrian van den, 143, 205–6
Huit-clos (No Exit), 54
Humanism, 171
Humanistic, 126
Husserl, Edmund, 25, 159
Hype and Cool, 61
Hyperbolic, 39
Ideal, 39, 82, 95, 111, 113, 120, 123, 126, 174, 192
  Idealist, 43
  Idealistic, 124–25, 144
Ideology, 39–40, 51
Idiosyncrasies, 38
Individual, 25, 34, 36, 42, 47, 51, 60–64, 78, 80, 82–83, 88, 96–99, 101, 104, 106–7, 114–16, 118–19, 127–30, 140, 142, 148–53, 156–64, 167, 169, 171, 173–75, 180, 182–87, 192, 194
In-itself, 62, 99, 140, 159, 162, 164
Intellectual, 1, 3–5, 7, 12–14, 16, 22, 24–25, 28, 30–33, 36, 38–39, 44, 48, 53, 80, 89–90, 92, 94, 97–98, 100, 102, 108, 111–12, 128, 131,

141, 145–47, 167, 169, 182, 188, 191, 193, 195, 197, 201–2, 204
Intellectually, 21, 33
Intelligentsia, 58
Invasion, 46
Jealousy, 24
Jean-Baptiste (see: Sartre)
Jean-Paul-Charles-Aymard-Léon-Eugène, 10, 15, 17, 20, 30, 50
Jeune, 15
Jewish, 30–31, 36
Journalist, 49–50, 77
Judaken, Jonathan, 31
Kant, Emmanuel, 80
Kantian, 81
L'anglaise, 16
Legacy, 2–3, 14, 35, 89, 97, 143, 165–66, 178, 191–92, 207
Levy, Benny, 124, 193
Liberté, 19
Lifetime, 7, 102
Linsenbard, Gail Evelyn, 134
Lisa, Appignanesi, 24
Literary, 2–3, 7, 10, 25–28, 32–34, 36, 38–40, 44, 49, 52, 54, 57–58, 60, 72–73, 83, 86–87, 89–90, 97, 101, 104, 112, 118, 123–25, 131–33, 140, 142–45, 159, 167, 190–94, 202–3, 205, 207
Literary accomplishments, 32, 39
Literary career, 54, 112, 123, 144
Literary circles, 34, 72, 90
Literary contribution, 28, 36, 101, 104, 124, 167, 192, 202
Literary critique, 193
Literary discipline, 3, 125, 132, 205
Literary expertise, 73
Literary history, 26, 57, 142, 159, 205
Literary intelligentsia, 58
Literary legacy, 2–3, 89, 97, 192
Literary project, 118, 131, 133, 190
Literary prowess, 7, 25
Literary stardom, 10, 44, 60, 207
Literary successes, 27
Literary talent, 49
Literary talents, 33
Literary tentacles, 143

Literary valor, 83
Literary wealth, 191
Literary work, 34, 54, 58, 133, 145, 194
Literature, 2, 5, 7, 12, 19, 31–35, 37, 39, 48, 56, 59, 65, 72, 74, 82, 87, 93, 95, 101, 108, 118–20, 122, 131, 134, 145, 182, 187–88, 191–92, 195–96, 202–3
Louis-le-Grand, 21
Lycée, 21, 25, 30
Lycée condorcet, 30
Lycée henri iv, 21
L'enfance d'un chef, 20
L'Existentialisme, 142
Magazine, 58
Mann, Anika, 182–83
Maria, Pramaggiore, 23
Mariam, Fraser, 23
Mark, Poster, 50
Marriage, 24, 186
Marx, Karl, 80
Marxism, 50, 206
Marxist, 50
Materialistic, 124–25
Materials, 5, 7, 44, 88–89, 110–11, 126, 190, 206–7, 209
Mauvaise, 64, 162
Mauvaise foi, 162
Maxims, 148, 172
McEwen, Todd, 91
Merleau-Ponty, Maurice, 58
Meszaros, Istvan, 109–10
Metaethics, 70, 75–77
Meteorologist, 46
Militaire, 45
Military, 12, 42–47, 53
Modus, 172
Moliere, 91
Mont-parnasse, 17
Moral, 2–4, 6, 12–13, 51, 67, 72–77, 79, 82–83, 86, 89–90, 92–93, 95, 97–101, 103–4, 109, 111–13, 117, 119, 124, 130, 134, 137, 140, 143–44, 146, 148–50, 159, 168, 172, 174, 177–78, 180, 186, 190–92, 195–97, 202–4, 207–8
Morale, 110, 112, 177

Index

Moralist (see: Sartre)
Morality, 37, 51, 65, 67, 70, 75–76, 79–80, 87–88, 90, 93–96, 102, 104, 113, 119–20, 123, 127, 140, 144–50, 156, 158–59, 163, 166, 171–74, 183, 194, 196–97
Morals, 148, 172
Narvez, Darcia, 76
Nausea, 32, 54
Nausée, 32, 54
Nazi, 49, 52
Nazi germany, 52
Nazi occupation, 49
Néant, 54
Nobel, 19, 28, 39–40
Nobelprize, 39
Non-academic, 5
Non-being, 140, 142, 151, 161, 163
Non-positional, 152
Normative, 70, 75, 77
Normative ethics, 70, 75, 77
Norms, 77, 98, 101, 149
Norms and values, 98
Norms of conducts, 77
Nothingness, 30, 46, 49–50, 53–54, 62, 99–100, 109–10, 112–13, 116–17, 119, 124, 142, 159–60, 164, 176–77, 203, 207
Novelist (see: Sartre)
Nurse, 19
Object, 117, 151, 159
Objectification, 116
Objectivist, 183, 186
Objectivity, 76
Object-ness, 116–17
Objects, 116, 132
Omnipresent, 123, 175, 207
One-self, 107
Ontological, 36, 62, 106–7, 113, 115, 118, 130, 142, 159, 182, 184
Ontology, 3, 5, 38, 61, 64, 71, 74–75, 78, 96–98, 100, 104, 110, 112–15, 118, 120, 126, 137, 140, 142, 146, 151, 169, 171, 175, 177, 185, 190, 193–94, 197, 207–9
Open-ended, 22, 36
Oppressed-oppressor, 184
Oppression, 52, 183

Oppressor, 52, 183–84
Optimistic message, 171
Ownership, 83, 95
O'Neil, Patrick M., 52, 59
Paris, 15, 21, 25, 30–31, 47, 49, 112
Pedophile, 91
Pellauer, David, 176–78, 203–4
Phenomenology, 5, 25, 29–30, 51, 61, 74, 95, 106, 109, 112, 123, 131, 151, 159, 164, 193, 208–9
Philanderer, 91
Philosopher, 1, 3–4, 12–13, 15, 34, 36, 38, 40, 51, 71–72, 80, 83, 90, 97, 100, 103, 113, 141–43, 168, 177, 190, 197, 202, 204, 207–8
Philosophy, 2, 4–6, 11–14, 21, 25–26, 31–34, 36, 38, 55, 59–62, 64, 67, 72–75, 78–79, 82–83, 86, 89–90, 94, 96–98, 101, 105, 107–9, 111, 117, 120, 123–24, 128, 130–32, 134–35, 137, 139, 142–44, 146–47, 150–51, 156, 167, 169–71, 173, 175, 178, 182, 186, 188–92, 194–97, 203, 208
Phobia, 35
Physical, 63–64, 96, 159
Physiologically, 129
Plays, 44, 48–50, 54, 115, 150, 174, 180
Playwright, 30, 42, 49, 54
Polemicist, 32
Politics, 12, 31, 42, 50–51, 53, 76
Political, 1, 7, 10, 30, 34, 41, 43–44, 49–53, 58
Politically, 49–50, 53
Politicians, 77
Posthumes, 34, 36
Posthumous, 36, 83, 88, 102, 133–34, 168
Postmortem, 94
Post-mortem, 1
Postwar, 50
Pramaggiore, Maria, 23
Praxis and action, 62
Priest, 159
Prolific, 50, 98, 122–23
Prolific novelist, 50
Prolific writer, 122–23

240

Protégé, 31
Protest, 53
Psychoanalysis, 99
Psychology, 12, 20, 60, 76, 205
Pundit, 2, 147, 168, 194, 204, 208
Puritan, 93
Radical, 12, 75, 145, 205
Ranwez, Alain, 26, 57–58, 142, 159, 205
Raymond, Aron, 58
Realistic, 124–25, 145
Revue, 58–59
Rituals, 106
Romanesque, 20
Romantic, 12, 19, 21–23, 77, 91–92
Romantic escapades, 91
Romantic relation, 21
Romantic relationship, 22
Rousseau, Jean Jacques, 80
Rowley, Hazel, 23, 91–92
Tete-a-Tete, 23, 91
Ryan, James Hugh, 33
Sabbaghi, Rachid, 32
Saint-Germain-des-Pres, 17
Sartre, 1–7, 9–25, 28–40, 42–54, 56–65, 67, 71–73, 81–83, 86, 88–113, 115–20, 122–35, 137, 140–53, 157–64, 166–72, 174–78, 181–86, 188–97, 200–209
Poulou (see: Sartre)
Sartrean ethics, 4–6, 13–14, 65, 67, 70–73, 81–83, 87–90, 92, 94, 97, 101–2, 108–11, 118, 120, 123–25, 130–32, 135, 140, 143–44, 168–69, 171, 173, 175–78, 181–82, 185–91, 193–97, 202, 204, 207–8
Sartrean legacy, 14, 89, 165
Sartrien, 82
Schrag, Calvin O., 51, 61, 109
Schweitzer, Anne-Marie, 15
Sedulous, 132
Self, 62, 64, 98, 153, 160, 186
Self-aware, 152
Self-awareness, 152
Self-consciousness, 152
Self-deceptions, 169
Self-identity, 40, 42, 62
Semantics, 100

Séquestrées, 52
Serendipitous, 146
Simont, Juliette, 34, 36
Stardom, 10, 44, 60, 207
Stone, 100, 187, 189, 203
Subject, 37, 44, 53, 65, 82, 109, 116, 133–34, 142, 151, 159, 161, 173, 192
Subjected, 52, 161, 183
Subjective, 82, 95, 100, 116, 142, 152, 161, 193, 195
Subjectivism, 186
Subjectivist, 186
Subjectivity, 76, 152, 161
Subjects, 1, 23, 90
Sumner, Leonard Wayne, 77
Symbiotic, 129, 166, 209
Tape-recorded, 124
Teacher, 25, 35
Trademark, 144
Trajectory, 10, 28–29, 44
Typifies, 63
Tyranny, 50
Unapologetic, 145
Unethical, 191, 209
Uniformity, 97
Unity, 147
Unwise, 125
Upbringing, 10, 17
Utilitarian, 80
Value, 75, 98–101, 104, 113, 115–16, 119, 127, 140, 148–50, 159, 163, 169, 174, 183, 186, 192–93
Velasquez, Manuel, 78
Vietnam, 12, 53
Virtue, 74, 76–77, 149, 172, 180
War, 12, 42–50, 53, 56, 59–60
Warburton, 171
Western, 11, 25, 34
Western philosophy, 11, 34
Wiley, John, 50
Woman, 20, 24, 30, 35, 80, 116
Womanizer, 23
Young, 15, 18, 20, 30–31, 45, 48
Young age, 20
Young fans, 31
Young poulou, 15
Young widow, 18

241

Index

Young woman, 30
Youth, 17, 43
Youthful men, 44
Zeal, 21
Zone, 19

ABOUT THE AUTHOR

BEN WOOD JOHNSON, Ph.D.

Dr. Johnson is a social observer. He is also a multidisciplinary scholar. He writes about Philosophy, Legal Theory, and Foreign Policy. He also writes about Education (School Leadership), Politics, Ethics, Race, and Crime.

Dr. Johnson is a Penn State graduate. He holds a Doctorate in Educational Administration and Leadership, a Master's degree in Political Science, a Master's degree in Public Administration, and a Bachelor's degree in Criminal Justice.

About the Author

Dr. Johnson worked in law enforcement. He attended John Jay College of Criminal Justice. He is fluent in many languages, including, but not limited to, English, French, Spanish, Portuguese, and Italian.

Dr. Johnson enjoys reading, poetry, painting, and music. You may contact Dr. Johnson by using the information listed below.

Other Info

Mailing/Postal Info:

Eduka Solutions
330 W. Main St #214
Middletown, PA 17057

Electronic Address:

E-mail Address: benwoodpost@gmail.com

Other Info:

Find the author (Ben Wood Johnson) on the following media platforms.

Other Info

Official Twitter handle: @benwoodpost

Official Facebook Page: @benwoodpost

Websites:

Official blog (Ben Wood Post): www.benwoodpost.org

Official website: www.drbenwoodjohnson.com

Academic website: www.benwoodjohnson.com

You may sign up to receive regular updates about the author's academic activities

OTHER WORKS

Other works by Dr. Ben Wood Johnson include the following:
- Racism: What is it?
- Sartrean Ethics: A Defense of Jean-Paul Sartre as a Moral Philosopher
- Sartre Lives On
- Forced Out of Vietnam: A Policy Analysis of the Fall of Saigon
- Natural Law: Morality and Obedience
- Cogito Ergo Philosophus

Other Works

- Le Racisme et le Socialisme: La Discrimination Raciale dans un Milieu Capitaliste
- International Law: The Rise of Russia as a Global Threat
- Être Noir: Quel Malheur!
- L'homme et le Racisme: Être Responsable de vos Actions et Omissions
- Pennsylvania Inspired Leadership : A Roadmap for American Educators
- Adult Education in America: A Policy Assessment of Adult Learning
- Striving to Survive: The Human Migration Story
- Postcolonial Africa: Three Comparative Essays about the African State

TESKO

www.ingramcontent.com/pod-product-compliance
Lightning Source LLC
Chambersburg PA
CBHW022000100426
42738CB00042B/998